W9-BKX-753

Teaching Writing
to Visual, Auditory, and Kinesthetic Learners

For Sam

Teaching Writing
to Visual, Auditory, and
Kinesthetic Learners

LIBRARY
FRANKLIN PIERCE COLLEGE
RINDGE, NH 03461

DONOVAN R. WALLING

CORWIN PRESS
A SAGE Publications Company
Thousand Oaks, California

Copyright © 2006 by Corwin Press

All rights reserved. When forms and sample documents are included, their use is authorized only by educators, local school sites, and/or noncommercial or nonprofit entities who have purchased the book. Except for that usage, no part of this book may be reproduced or utilized in any form or by any means, electronic or mechanical, including photocopying, recording, or by any information storage and retrieval system, without permission in writing from the publisher.

For information:

Corwin Press
A Sage Publications Company
2455 Teller Road
Thousand Oaks, California 91320
E-mail: order@corwinpress.com

Sage Publications Ltd.
1 Oliver's Yard
55 City Road
London EC1Y 1SP
United Kingdom

Sage Publications India Pvt. Ltd.
B-42, Panchsheel Enclave
Post Box 4109
New Delhi 110 017 India

Printed in the United States of America.

Library of Congress Cataloging-in-Publication Data

Walling, Donovan R., 1948-
Teaching writing to visual, auditory, and kinesthetic learners / Donovan R. Walling.
    p. cm.
Includes bibliographical references and index.
ISBN 1-4129-2519-3 (cloth) — ISBN 1-4129-2520-7 (pbk.)
    1. Composition (Language arts) 2. Perceptual learning. 3. Active learning.
4. Individualized instruction. I. Title.
LB1575.8.W37 2006
808'.042071—dc22   2005029173

This book is printed on acid-free paper.

06   07   08   09   10   11   9   8   7   6   5   4   3   2   1

Acquisitions Editor:	Faye Zucker
Editorial Assistant:	Gem Rabanera
Project Editor:	Tracy Alpern
Copy Editor:	Tom Lacey
Proofreader:	Caryne Brown
Typesetter:	C&M Digitals (P) Ltd.
Indexer:	Gloria Tierney
Cover Designer:	Rose Storey

Contents

Acknowledgments   ix

About the Author   xi

Introduction   1

1. **Writing Processes and Differentiated Instruction**   **5**
   Assembly-Line Writing   6
   Teaching Writing for Meaning   7
   Learning Styles and Differentiated Instruction   8
   Stimulus, Process, and Product   10
   Learning Styles Self-Assessment   13
   References   17

2. **Writing About Real Things**   **19**
   School Writing Versus Authentic Writing   20
   Multidimensional Authentic Response Writing   21
   And Then: The Process Phase   23
   Pathways to Fluency   27
   Sample Lesson 2.1: Respond as a ___ Might   28
   Sample Lesson 2.2: Multidimensional
       Authentic Response Writing   30
   References   31

3. **Observing, Then Writing**   **33**
   Sensory Reportage   33
   Visual Reportage   35
   Auditory Reportage   35
   Kinesthetic Reportage   37
   Translation Into Different Forms   38
   Sense Exploration   39
   Writing Up the Taxonomy   42
   Sample Lesson 3.1: Template and Checklist Strategies   43

Sample Lesson 3.2: Observation and Sensory Reportage   45
References   46

4. Organizing Artistically   **47**
Pearls-on-a-String Organization   47
Inductive and Deductive Organization   50
Inverted Pyramid Organization   53
Identifying Key Ideas   55
Another Translation: Factual Reportage   57
Sample Lesson 4.1: Gathering
    and Organizing Information   58
Sample Lesson 4.2: Artistic Organization   59

5. Clarifying Ideas Using Walkabout Strategies   **61**
Walkabouts   62
Paragraph Walkabouts   65
Auditory and Kinesthetic Paragraph Walkabouts   67
Collaborative Planning, Drafting, and Revising   68
Guide on the Side   70
Sample Lesson 5.1: Paragraph
    Walkabout and Sense Exploration   71
Sample Lesson 5.2: Paragraph Walkabout Analysis   73

6. Using Patterns and Rhythms for Writing Sense   **75**
Discerning and Adjusting Patterns and Rhythms   76
Translating the Visual and the
    Auditory for Kinesthetic Learning   80
Brevity, Elaboration, and Conceptual Density   81
Outlining to Revise   83
Sample Lesson 6.1: Outlining to Revise—and Revising   85
Sample Lesson 6.2: Patterns
    and Rhythms for Writing Sense   87

7. Choosing the Right Words   **89**
Basic Words: Nouns and Verbs   89
Correct and Politically Correct   91
More Basic Words: Adjectives and Adverbs   95
Brevity   97
Spelling Improvement   99
Sample Lesson 7.1: Reviewing the Words   100
Sample Lesson 7.2: Up Close—Choosing
    the Right Words   101
References   102

8. **Increasing Focused Engagement**   **103**
    Selective Correction   104
    The Importance of Portfolios   106
    Making and Using Rubrics   108
    Rubrics and the SAT Essay   111
    Concluding Thoughts and a Final Checklist   112
    References   113

Resources   **115**
    Print   115
    Online   116

Index   **117**

Acknowledgments

The author wishes to acknowledge the inspiration and ideas provided over many years by friends and colleagues in the Sheboygan Area School District in Wisconsin, in particular Dr. Wayne Homstad, now assistant professor of education at Lakeland College.

Corwin Press would like to thank the following reviewers for their contribution to this book:

Marilee Sprenger, Educational Consultant, Seattle Pacific University, Seattle, WA

Erin Sullivan, Research Associate, National Research Center on the Gifted and Talented, University of Connecticut, Storrs, CT

Sue Teele, Director of Education Extension, University of California at Riverside, Riverside, CA

Carol Ann Tomlinson, Professor of Educational Leadership, University of Virginia, Charlottesville, VA

Pamela Fannin Wilkinson, Educational Consultant, The Winston School San Antonio, San Antonio, TX

About the Author

Donovan R. Walling is a writer, editor, and educator. He has taught art, English, and journalism in the United States and abroad, and he has served as a curriculum administrator in public school districts in Wisconsin and Indiana. Currently, he is director of publications at Phi Delta Kappa International, the professional association in education. He is the author or editor of twelve professional books for educators and numerous articles and other publications. His most recent books are *Visual Knowing: Connecting Art and Ideas Across the Curriculum* (Corwin Press, 2005) and *Public Education, Democracy, and the Common Good* (Phi Delta Kappa Educational Foundation, 2004). He is nationally recognized in the field of art education, where his publications also include the Corwin Press book, *Rethinking How Art Is Taught: A Critical Convergence* (2000), the core chapter on visual and performing arts for the Association for Supervision and Curriculum Development's *Curriculum Handbook* (2002), and the "Art in the Schools" entry for Macmillan's *Encyclopedia of Education* (2003).

Introduction

This book focuses on teaching writing to visual, auditory, and kinesthetic learners, who usually are not natural writers. Research has established that students of all ages construct knowledge in a variety of ways, based in large part on how their brains process stimuli. The ways that students' minds work also influence how—and how well—they learn to write. Teachers who understand that students respond in different ways to various types of stimuli can differentiate writing instruction according to students' preferred learning styles and thus increase students' success.

Some students process stimuli most effectively using linguistic cues. These students often are early readers and, later on, can be the natural writers in the class, those students who acquire writing competence seemingly without much effort. Other students rely on logical or mathematical cues to discern information and construct understandings. These students also may be able to acquire writing skills with relative ease. Students whose minds work in these linguistic and logical ways generally have the easiest time in school, particularly in academic classes, for the simple reason that most academic teaching is based on using linguistic and logical-mathematical stimuli that match these learning styles.

However, many students do not construct knowledge most effectively in these ways. Visual learners respond most strongly not to information that they read or hear, but to information that they see, such as pictures and patterns. Auditory learners respond to information that they hear, such as spoken language, music, and rhythms. And kinesthetic learners learn most easily through movement and physical activity.

All of that said, of course, no student uses only one mode of response—or learning style—to the exclusion of all others. But from students' early grades onward, teachers can observe how they learn most easily and effectively by noticing students' dominant learning styles, if any. They can observe whether students learn better from reading (linguistic), looking at pictures (visual), listening (auditory), or doing physical activities (kinesthetic). Observant teachers often notice that their visual, auditory, and kinesthetic students struggle with learning how to express ideas and concepts in writing. These learners can be "picture smart," "music smart," and "body smart," but they may be challenged in the classroom because instruction and assessment are structured in ways that require performance tasks and reward evidence that learners are "word smart" and "number smart."

My purpose in this book is to offer a useful instructional perspective and practical strategies that teachers can use to help their visual, auditory, and kinesthetic learners become effective writers. The visual and performing arts draw heavily on these modes of learning and so, for the sake of convenience, I occasionally use the term *artistic mind* in this book to characterize, collectively, the essential mental processes that these students use to construct knowledge, including learning how to write.

Put another way: Writing is most often taught in schools as a linear process, which best suits the linguistic-logical learner. Those who approach writing with an artistic mind-set, however, often approach writing in nonlinear ways. If all learners—including those whose learning styles stress visual, auditory, and kinesthetic strengths—are to be taught to write well, then both linear and nonlinear approaches should be used. It may help to think of standard, linear writing instruction as the freeway: fast and sometimes ill suited to certain vehicles. Writing strategies for the artistic mind often need to take the back road, where there may be more to see and hear. The road will roll through hills and valleys, but the destination—the instructional goal—is the same: the development of effective writing skills.

The seeds of this book were planted by my teaching experiences that now stretch back more than three decades and have periodically germinated in articles and other publications, most notably a monograph that I wrote for Phi Delta Kappa Educational Foundation, *A Model for Teaching Writing: Process and Product* (1987). In that monograph I attempted to articulate in brief the need for teachers to approach the writing process as a collection of flexible, in some ways idiosyncratic processes—emphasis on the plural. Adopting this view permits teachers to see multiple pathways to writing success for students, an essential view if teachers are truly to address the learning needs of visual, auditory, and kinesthetic learners.

Books that teach writing using linear approaches are available already (see the Resources section for many excellent choices), and so this book is going to focus on nonlinear approaches to teaching writing. To be clear at the outset, this book is not about teaching creative writing, which usually means writing fiction or poetry. Nor is it about teaching personal narratives, although some are included as a basis for personal forms of nonfiction, such as personal-experience essays. This book is about essential, critical, and authentic literacy, forms of writing that demand both basic writing competence and higher-level thinking. This book is for teachers who want to teach all of the learners in their classrooms how to:

- observe and report their observations in writing,
- synthesize diverse viewpoints in writing,
- frame logical arguments in writing.

Such writing often can and should be creatively enhanced, but that is a secondary goal that follows only after the primary goals have been achieved.

Teachers who adopt strategies that better address the learning needs of artistically minded students will find that they have expanded their repertoire of effective teaching strategies for all students. Imparting new perspectives on teaching and learning will enhance the information-processing capabilities of their word- and number-smart students as well. The strategies in this book can be used at various grades from upper elementary through high school and into college, and many of these strategies also can be adapted for very young writers or for writers with learning disabilities.

Writing is an essential life skill that all students must master to succeed in school and to perform well in their careers. Writing is a core component of cognition. Externally, writing displays the writer's thoughts and provides evidence of learning. Internally, the act of writing helps the writer to form and clarify thoughts and to engage in higher-level cognitive processes, such as analysis and synthesis. It also propels the learner toward deeper reflection about content, process, experience, and mastery.

Clearly important in the context of school success is evidence suggesting that students who write well also perform better than poor writers on other measures of academic competence (e.g., White, 1999). Thus today's high-stakes testing environment in schools further increases the need for all students to learn how to write well. Many local and state competency assessments include writing components. In 2005 the College Board began to require an essay component as part of the revised SAT I examination. That writing test takes 50 to 60 minutes and demands that students write with some complexity in order to be successful.

Teaching Writing to Visual, Auditory, and Kinesthetic Learners should be read as a starting point for expanding the writing curriculum. Incorporating nontraditional instructional strategies will help teachers address the learning needs of artistically minded students. The goal for these students—and all students—is to become effective writers.

REFERENCES

Walling, D. R. (1987). *A model for teaching writing: Process and product.* Fastback 256. Bloomington, IN: Phi Delta Kappa Educational Foundation.

White, S. (1999). *The NAEP 1998 reading report card: National and state highlights.* (NCES 1999-479). Washington, DC: National Center for Education Statistics, U.S. Department of Education.

1 Writing Processes and Differentiated Instruction

Many people, including teachers, hold two major misconceptions about writing. The first is that writing is a *deliberate, linear process.* The second is that, because of the first misconception, writers should write in a deliberate, linear manner. Teachers who hold these misconceptions must teach their students to write in this way so that the students become successful writers. Quite the opposite result occurs. This narrow, one-dimensional view of how writing happens hampers instruction and prevents many students from learning to write well. Thus, at the outset, it makes sense to set the record straight about writing processes—in the plural form of the word—and about how a multidimensional view of writing can lay a foundation for differentiating writing instruction, especially for students who are visual, auditory, or kinesthetic learners.

Visual, *auditory*, and *kinesthetic* are the identifiers that I will use throughout this book to designate learning styles that are dominant for certain students. Most researchers also would note that a student's preferred learning style, or styles, may be situation- or topic-specific. In other words, the student may be an effective linguistic learner when confronted with certain information but may learn more effectively using visual or auditory approaches when confronted with other information. Therefore, these identifiers should be viewed as cues to guide the teacher in thinking about instruction and in differentiating instructional strategies to help students work to their strengths, but not as learning labels for students.

ASSEMBLY-LINE WRITING

Linear and *deliberate* may not be commonplace descriptors, but they also are useful. These terms describe how many people think about writing, even though they may use other words. *Linear* refers to the act in which the writer starts (or should start) with an idea, takes pen in hand or taps on a keyboard, and winds up with that very idea set down in a predetermined form—as a poem, a story, an essay, or some other product. *Deliberate* implies that the writer does not (and should not) stray from the path to this product destination. The idea must never change, nor should its intended form. An essay may not transform itself into a story or a poem; it must remain an essay. This is assembly-line writing. Adopting this view of how writing happens forces the writer into the role of an assembly-line worker, one who takes an idea and moves it along the line through a series of pre-set actions that will result in an acceptable product.

Does this process work? Can a writer produce a successful piece of writing in this manner? The answer to both questions, of course, is yes. For some writing and for some writers, this is the most effective process to use. But it will not work for all writing or all writers. It may not work even for most writing or most writers. And it will not serve all students when used as the philosophy undergirding writing instruction, especially when the students are visual, auditory, or kinesthetic learners.

In the past 25 years, the writing process in most classrooms from elementary school through college has become institutionalized. Few teachers have escaped the drill that writing should be taught as a process, and the steps in this process are well known: prewriting, drafting, editing, revising, rewriting—with a few variations. This approach was proposed as a more productive alternative to teaching writing by merely assigning a topic and then correcting (or beating until it bled) the student's written work with the notion that the student would then take the piece back and improve it. A great deal of ink was spilled over the distinction between the old instructional mode of assigning writing (and leaving it to the student to figure out a successful process for achieving a good result) and the new mode of teaching writing as a process.

Although process writing, as it came to be called, was proposed with the notion of having flexibility built in, some teachers and textbook publishers leaped at the chance to codify the process, inadvertently rendering it rigid and rote. The writing process is a formula, and the formula works reasonably well for students when they are expected to produce formulaic writing, often the kind that is expected on standardized tests. In the current atmosphere of high-stakes testing, this instructional course of action can be seductive. After all, it is difficult to argue with rote writing if teaching students to write in this manner works to ensure test success. On the other hand, rigidly conceived process-writing instruction garners criticism as yet another form of teaching to the test, something that curriculum theorists and practitioners agree tends almost always to narrow the curriculum and to reduce real learning.

TEACHING WRITING FOR MEANING

The effective teacher knows that spelling taught by rote is useful only for passing the test on a Friday. Indeed, an all-too-common lament is that students do not spell the same words correctly in their written work that they do spell correctly on a weekly test. There is little automatic transference of spelling skill from the one situation to the other. Transference skills must be deliberately taught. Some good rote spellers may become spelling bee champions. But most students lose words learned by rote unless they take other actions to make the words useful, such as defining them, using them in meaningful sentences and stories, talking about them, and so on. The process of constructing new knowledge, along with the ability to use that knowledge in various new contexts, simply takes more than mere memorization. The same can be said for writing.

Students who learn the typical process-writing formula can reproduce it when called on to do so for a writing test. Doing so will achieve success if that is what the test requires. But not all tests require only that. The formula will not produce successful writers per se if success is defined as the ability to take an idea and truly work with it to produce a thoughtful, original piece of writing—in other words, to write for meaning. Passing a test is important, but the larger goal is learning to write well. When it is reached, passing the test becomes automatic.

An apt characterization of deliberate, linear writing is *transcription*, the simple transfer of an idea from the writer's mind directly onto the page. Transcription is a useful skill, and it should be taught. But it is not all that should be taught. Transcription is to writing what addition is to computation, a tiny (albeit important) part of it. Real writing—complex, meaningful writing—is akin to calculus. I will argue throughout this book that all students can become better writers if teachers attend to writing instruction as multidimensional and nonformulaic. Even students who seem to be natural writers, who learn effortlessly how to write well, will be better served by instructional approaches that also accommodate the visual, auditory, and kinesthetic learning styles of students who are less likely to be natural writers.

Only some writing is best created in a plodding, straight-line sort of way. And only some writers should write in this way, and then only for specific purposes. Visual, auditory, and kinesthetic learners need to approach writing with the understanding that their initial idea likely will change shape as they write. And all writers can benefit from the creative wrestling that such a premise entails. Ideas are malleable and slippery, shape-shifters that mutate as we think about them. The most effective writing processes are thoughtful and open, admitting and embracing the slipperiness of ideas. The most successful writing usually results after trials, errors, and corrections.

An idea with which a writer begins may look very different by the time the writer finally sets it down on paper. The writer may try out one way of writing about the idea, have a new thought, and go back to start again. The process may include rethinking, replanning, crossing-out, and rewriting in any number of ways. The student writer, like the successful adult writer, must be free to shape and reshape the work repeatedly if that is what is needed to produce an effectively written piece. And even this final product may be more like a pencil sketch than a bronze sculpture. An idea on paper is still an idea: still malleable, still slippery. Any number of writers take up pieces that they supposedly have finished and rework them weeks, months, or even years later. Walt Whitman was notorious for tinkering with his published poems before they were reprinted in later editions. During his lifetime, *Leaves of Grass* was perpetually in progress. It went through eight editions between the original publication in 1855 and the final one in 1891, issued shortly before Whitman's death the following year.

Allowing and encouraging students to explore all the byways on the road to a product is contrary to the notion that writing is a deliberate, linear process. But it is more often the way in which real writers work, and the goal of writing instruction should be to produce students who can write as real writers do, not merely as automatons who can pass tests. Real writers also can pass tests—and they can do much more.

LEARNING STYLES AND DIFFERENTIATED INSTRUCTION

Stanford University professor Eliot Eisner (1983) points out that teachers who truly master the art of teaching are those willing to build a continuously expanding repertoire of instructional strategies in order to teach all learners most effectively. Teachers who understand the dynamics of learning styles can tailor instruction that will bring out the best efforts of students learning to write. The strategies explored in the chapters that follow focus on visual, auditory, and kinesthetic learning styles—in other words, styles related to sensory stimuli.

Education consultant Marilee Sprenger (2003) writes of "differentiation through sensory pathways," using "visual," "auditory/verbal," and "kinesthetic/tactile" as descriptors of ways (paths) by which students take in information or process sensory stimuli. Scientific theorists believe that the human brain differentiates such stimuli to understand them. She explains:

> Each sense has a passageway. The thalamus sorts information and sends it to the top layer of the brain, the neocortex. The neocortex has an area for each type of sensory stimuli. The visual cortex processes visual information, the auditory cortex processes sounds, and the somatic cortex processes touch. The information from each is then sent to the rhinal cortex. Here the senses are put back together into one representation. (p. 35)

This basic biomechanical information is helpful in understanding why providing stimuli according to a student's dominant sensory pathway can affect learning.

Brain theory, however, is only one of many learning theories that point in the same general direction—toward identifying students' preferred learning style, or styles, and then structuring teaching to match. Educator and author Gayle Gregory (2005) is particularly helpful in identifying a number of theoretical and philosophical formulations that can help teachers understand the need to differentiate instruction according to students' learning styles from various points of view. Gregory points to the work of researchers in psychology and education such as Carl Jung, Anthony Gregorc, David Kolb, Bernice McCarthy, Don Lowry, Richard Strong, Harvey Silver, and J.R. Hanson.

Gregory also identifies Guild and Garger's (1985) four modes of thinking—cognition, conceptualizing, affect, and behavior—as a useful framework that teachers can use when considering how to differentiate instruction to meet students' learning needs. These modes can each be characterized by a question:

- *Cognition:* How do I know?
- *Conceptualization:* How do I think?
- *Affect:* How do I decide?
- *Behavior:* How do I act?

According to Gregory, "In most cases, learners will have a dominant style within a mode that is visual, auditory, or tactile/kinesthetic" (p. 25).

Gregory also links differentiation of instruction to theories of intelligence, including Art Costa and Bena Kallick's (2000) "12 intelligent behaviors,"

Howard Gardner's (1983, 1999) "multiple intelligences," and Robert Sternberg's (1996) "triarchic intelligence model." Within Costa and Kallick's models of behavior (persistence, questioning, metacognition, and others) reside the ways in which students go about persisting, questioning, and so on, some of them being visual, auditory, and kinesthetic. Similarly, Gardner's intelligences specifically speak to ways of processing stimuli in intelligences that are verbal/linguistic, musical/rhythmic, visual/spatial, and bodily/kinesthetic. And finally, visual, auditory, and kinesthetic (and other) learning-style preferences reside within Sternberg's delineations of practical, analytical, and creative intelligences.

This overview barely touches on the myriad underpinnings of learning-style theories. Even so, it should be easy to see that if teachers want all students to learn how to write well, it will be necessary to develop a differentiated or multidimensional approach to teaching writing processes—again with an emphasis on there being more than one process—that will match students' learning styles.

STIMULUS, PROCESS, AND PRODUCT

Let's go back to writing instruction in particular. A helpful way to think about writing processes is to consider how writing really happens. Conceptually, there are three phases: stimulus, process, and product. Figure 1.1 shows these phases as a sort of arrow. The head of the arrow is marked off by a dotted line to indicate that the continuum of phases may or may not repeat as the writer develops the written work.

While this three-phase model is neater than most writing, it provides a general idea of how the act of writing usually proceeds. What actually happens as the writer moves through each phase reflects the idiosyncrasies of the writer. These idiosyncrasies embody the learning styles of the writer.

Stimulus

Writers do not produce writing out of thin air, and ideas do not arise from spontaneous generation. Students write on topics they are assigned or in response to thought, conversation, observation, reading, playing, or some other initial spark that lights the creative fire. I use the term *creative* here in its broad sense, meaning the urge to create a piece of writing in some form, not necessarily creative writing as it usually is characterized. Such a stimulus may be anything but esoteric. Students write in response

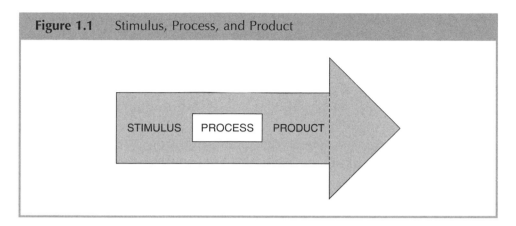

Figure 1.1   Stimulus, Process, and Product

SOURCE: An early version of this figure was included in Walling, D. R. (1987). *A Model for Teaching Writing: Process and Product.* Fastback 256. Bloomington, IN: Phi Delta Kappa Educational Foundation. Used with permission.

to teachers' assignments, just as adult news reporters, columnists, and business writers write in response to assignments made by their supervisors. The student's assignment may come in the context of a classroom project, or it may be a test prompt.

Students who feel drawn to writing will respond to self-selected stimuli. They may write notes to one another, letters and e-mail to family and friends, stories, poems, and scripts. They may keep a diary or journal. These students will benefit from multidimensional writing instruction, but they are already headed for writing success. They have demonstrated self-motivation to write. A multidimensional instructional approach will give them additional tools for expression that will enhance their ability to write.

On the other hand, some of their peers will not be stimulated to write. They may be moved to respond to stimuli in other ways, such as by drawing, singing, dancing, or acting. These are the visual, auditory, and kinesthetic learners who are the focus of this book. If these students are to learn how to write well, the teacher must meet the challenge of finding ways of helping them use their preferred learning styles, which may not include written expression.

Process

Another way of stating that last point is that the teacher must help visual, auditory, and kinesthetic learners use their talents and interests in ways that support the act of writing. The process phase can be divided into mental and physical components. If we were to characterize the shaft of the arrow in Figure 1.1 as a kind of highway with two lanes, one mental and one physical, then we might also envision that the writer/driver on this highway from stimulus to product should be free to change lanes at will.

The mental component includes activities such as brainstorming, analyzing, rehearsing, organizing, and evaluating. The physical component includes activities such as writing or keyboarding, acting out, talking to oneself or others, moving about, drawing, or other physical responses to the stimulus and to the mental component of process. The writer/driver on this highway might even straddle the line, so to speak, as in stream-of-consciousness writing, when thoughts are recorded as they occur to the writer.

Much of the later chapters of this book will be devoted to exploring how teachers can use a variety of instructional strategies to help visual, auditory, and kinesthetic learners—and all learners—fully explore processes that will result in the development of successful writing.

Product

The term *product* in this context means a piece of writing, not necessarily a finished composition. The product may be merely notes or random jottings. It may be an outline or a list of ideas, a word map or graphic organizer, a diagram or graph. Whatever form it takes, this piece of writing is the tangible, recorded response to the process phase. Indeed, if the process has been captured visually, that visual component can be described. If the process has been recorded aurally, then it can be transcribed.

If the product is a finished piece of writing—by whatever agreed-on standard constitutes *finished*—then that is the end of the highway, the dotted line on the arrow shaft in Figure 1.1. If the product, such as a graphic organizer or an outline, is an intermediate step, then the product continues as the arrow tip, pointing to a new stimulus for the next cycle of development. As this recycling occurs, Figure 1.1 expands to look more like the standard recycling symbol (see Figure 1.2). Each intermediate product becomes the stimulus for another process component, which leads to another product. This product also may be either intermediate, continuing the cycle, or final.

Writers, whether they are students or mature writers, will develop the final piece of writing through fewer or more cycles, depending on the processes they choose (or are encouraged) to employ and the nature of the final product they want to create. And so at some point the recycling will end—unless, like Walt Whitman, the writer chooses to revisit a work even after publication.

Figure 1.2 Recycling

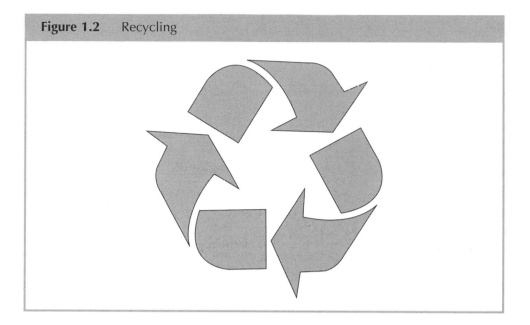

LEARNING STYLES SELF-ASSESSMENT

One way to set the stage for multidimensional writing instruction is to help students gain a sense of their preferred learning styles. Students who struggle with writing often are not aware that they may be approaching the act of writing in ways that are counterproductive. Their teachers may be frustrated as well because they do not know how to help them in their struggles. For example, if a student says, "I can't follow an outline. I always think of new things as I write that aren't in my outline," then the student probably is not going to experience success using a strategy that is essentially linear-logical. The simple, but wrong, answer is, "Do a better outline." The outline is not the real problem; using the wrong process strategy is. This student may need to brainstorm a graphic organizer, rather than an outline, as a starting point.

"But," the teacher may protest, "I'm supposed to teach students how to make an outline." Starting with an alternative is not to say that an outline might not be useful to the student or should not be taught, but an outline might be better employed as a way to analyze the organization of a draft later in the writing process. There is no rule that a traditional outline must be used as a starting point. If the teacher's goal is to teach outlining, that goal can still be accomplished by using a formal outline at the revision stage, rather than at the planning stage. (More about this strategy in Chapter 6.)

Figure 1.3 Student Learning Style Self-Assessment

Learning Styles Self-Assessment Inventory

I like to:	No (0)	Sometimes (1)	Often (2)	Usually (3)	Always (4)
1. keep a journal					
2. write letters or e-mail friends					
3. create sculptures					
4. do math					
5. solve puzzles					
6. make schedules or timelines					
7. listen to music					
8. play an instrument or sing					
9. record sound effects					
10. read and follow maps					
11. write stories or poems					
12. draw maps or house plans					
13. make designs					
14. play chess or checkers					
15. dance					
16. play a team sport					
17. paint or draw pictures					
18. do experiments with plants					
19. knit or weave					
20. work in a group					
21. help friends with problems					
22. tutor a classmate					
23. read books					
24. discuss social issues					
25. give directions					
26. take care of someone					
27. think about my goals					

Figure 1.3 (Continued)

I like to:	No (0)	Sometimes (1)	Often (2)	Usually (3)	Always (4)
28. cook and prepare meals					
29. write about my life					
30. draw or paint self-portraits					
31. ride a bicycle					
32. grow plants					
33. work in a garden					
34. study animals					
35. go on hikes					
36. act in skits and plays					
37. write music					
38. take care of a pet					
39. go fishing or hunting					
40. sing for myself or others					

Items Keyed to Visual, Auditory, and Kinesthetic Learning Style Categories:
Visual: 3, 5, 10, 12, 13, 14, 17, 30
Auditory: 7, 8, 9, 24, 36, 37, 40
Kinesthetic: 3, 15, 16, 19, 28, 31, 33, 35, 36, 39

Scoring Directions:
To compute the ratings for each category, add together the ratings for each item in the category and divide by the number of items in the category. The higher the average rating, the more likely that a visual, auditory, or kinesthetic intelligence or learning style will influence a student's success.

Copyright © 2006 by Corwin Press. All rights reserved. Reprinted from *Teaching Writing to Visual, Auditory, and Kinesthetic Learners*, by Donovan R. Walling. Thousand Oaks, CA: Corwin Press, www.corwinpress.com. Reproduction authorized only for the local school site or nonprofit organization that has purchased this book.

As teachers think about how to approach writing instruction in ways best suited to visual, auditory, and kinesthetic learners, a useful starting point is some form of student self-assessment of preferred learning styles. Figure 1.3 offers an example that can be used across a broad range of ages and grades, from upper elementary grades through high school.

This learning styles self-assessment inventory is not intended to be rigorously scientific. Rather it is meant to serve as an instructional tool and

Figure 1.4 Self-Assessment Response Form for Young Students

Directions: The teachers should read aloud a selection of the items, from the Learning Styles Self-Assessment Inventory. Students mark their responses by circling a smiley face, indicating whether they dislike, are neutral about, or like the activity. Below is a sample twenty-item response form.

1	☹	😐	☺
2	☹	😐	☺
3	☹	😐	☺
4	☹	😐	☺
5	☹	😐	☺
6	☹	😐	☺
7	☹	😐	☺
8	☹	😐	☺
9	☹	😐	☺
10	☹	😐	☺
11	☹	😐	☺
12	☹	😐	☺
13	☹	😐	☺
14	☹	😐	☺
15	☹	😐	☺
16	☹	😐	☺
17	☹	😐	☺
18	☹	😐	☺
19	☹	😐	☺
20	☹	😐	☺

can be readily adapted to work with younger students or adults. The idea behind using an inventory of this type is that, for students and teachers alike, making activities visible that are associated with how students learn best is educationally valuable. Humans willingly engage in activities they like, and they like those that they are somehow satisfied by, usually because they produce feelings of success or accomplishment. The inventory can be viewed from a general learning perspective or directly associated with visual, auditory, and kinesthetic learning styles. (For two other learning-style surveys for students, see Gregory, 2005, pp. 28–33.)

The inventory also can be shortened or lengthened provided that at least the targeted learning-style categories are included. Figure 1.3 shows how to group the items related to visual, auditory, and kinesthetic learning styles, as those are the target styles for this book. Other, more adult activities can be substituted in the inventory for work with adult literacy classes, for example. Teachers of younger students may want to shorten or simplify the inventory, and the youngest students might need to have the statements read aloud to them while they circle smiley faces (see Figure 1.4), instead of making check marks.

Using any self-assessment inventory proceeds from the notion that effective teaching requires that students and teachers work as partners. The teacher might determine which students learn better through visual strategies, for example, simply by observing the students in action and carefully analyzing their work. When students become involved in this assessment process, they discover information about their own learning. Such self-knowledge can be empowering, as the most successful students are those who at some point in their schooling take control of their own learning.

REFERENCES

Costa, A., & Kallick, B. (2000). *Habits of mind: A developmental series.* Alexandria, VA: Association for Supervision and Curriculum Development.

Eisner, E. (1983). The art and craft of teaching. *Educational Leadership, 40*(4), 4–13.

Gardner, H. (1983). *Frames of mind: The theory of multiple intelligences.* New York: Basic Books.

Gardner, H. (1999). *Intelligence reframed: Multiple intelligences for the 21st century.* New York: Basic Books.

Gregory, G. (2005). *Differentiating instruction with style: Aligning teacher and learner intelligences for maximum achievement.* Thousand Oaks, CA: Corwin.

Guild, P. B., & Garger, S. (1985). *Marching to different drummers.* Alexandria, VA: Association for Supervision and Curriculum Development.

Sprenger, M. (2003). *Differentiation through learning styles and memory.* Thousand Oaks, CA: Corwin.

Sternberg, R. (1996). *Successful intelligence.* New York: Simon & Schuster.

2 Writing About Real Things

In looking closely at the writing process and how instruction might best address the needs of visual, auditory, and kinesthetic learners, readers should remember that the focus of this book is nonfiction writing, whether cast as writing in school or authentic writing. These terms can be defined as follows: *School writing* is the general label used to describe writing found only or mostly in school assignments or on tests used in the classroom or standardized. The five-paragraph theme is an example of school writing; in fact, it is a cliché, which is not to say that it could not be useful as authentic writing. *Authentic writing* refers to writing that can be found anywhere, from a church bulletin to the *New York Times.* Authentic writing, in nonfiction terms, might be called *writing about real things.* Such writing accomplishes meaningful communication beyond the mere demonstration of writing skill, which often is the sole purpose of school writing. Authentic writing ranges from the step-by-step directions for building a model airplane to the critical review of a new motion picture.

Creative, as it applies to nonfiction writing, is another term that requires definition. Although many teachers use creative writing exclusively to mean fiction or poetry and not nonfiction, much of what is written about real things is highly creative or imaginative. Reality, after all, is the neighborhood where we all live, and it is full of interesting sights, sounds, and activities. Also in this neighborhood of real things are abstractions such as philosophical ideas and spiritual beliefs, which are certainly real even if they are intangible. Wars have been fought over ideas as often as for land or gold. Ideas are real in the way that X-rays are real. They become manifest in speech or on paper just as X-rays appear as images on a piece of film.

Understanding that school writing and authentic writing can be as creative as so-called creative writing is important because visual, auditory, and kinesthetic learners gravitate toward activities that are creative. These are learners who respond most positively on the learning styles self-assessment inventory (Figure 1.3) to statements such as "I like to play an instrument and sing," "I like to dance," and "I like to paint or draw pictures." They are motivated to express themselves through the arts—music, dance, theater, and the visual arts. If the teacher of writing can tap into this wellspring of motivation, these students likely will have greater success in learning how to write well—even when the vehicle for expression is nonfiction.

SCHOOL WRITING VERSUS AUTHENTIC WRITING

One of the ongoing professional debates in education centers on the relative merits of basal reading texts, which are contrived to fit students' perceived reading levels, and authentic, or found, texts such as trade books and stories in children's magazines. Each approach has its ardent supporters and its severe critics. But most teachers in the trenches realize that both types of text belong in the repertoire of effective strategies for reading instruction. The same can be said about school writing and authentic writing. Both can be instructionally effective.

School writing is distinguished by its elements of editorial control because writing assignments specify topic, form, length, and other characteristics. The merits of this form of controlled writing are several. It provides opportunities for the direct instruction of particular writing skills, permits students to collaborate within the same frame of reference, and offers the teacher a way to maintain curricular focus. Students in almost all schools—at almost all levels—will be expected to master certain aspects of school writing because it is the type of writing they will need to do on standardized tests. Increasingly, high-stakes testing is used to determine students' futures. Unfortunately, the controlled assignments used in school writing tend to limit opportunities for individual creative expression and may force all students to learn skills that some have already mastered, resulting in a loss of motivation. And so the teacher must find a tipping point and know when a controlled assignment will likely be most effective and when more freedom of choice and expression should be permitted.

Authentic writing is not the exact opposite of school writing, however, even though it can connote an anything-goes approach at times. Setting aside time for open writing is an example. Teachers who reserve time, daily or weekly, for independent writing permit students to choose to write a story, a poem, a script, a poster, or something similar. Authentic writing in this sense is writing that is entirely at the students' discretion, and it usually also is up to the students to share the written product or to keep it to themselves. But writing need not be quite so open in order to be authentic. Consider that adult workers in writing professions often proceed from an assignment, whether self-selected within certain limits or given directly to them by a supervisor. Media reporters may be assigned, for example, to cover city council meetings, or they may have a beat, a general area of reportage, from which they can choose the topics to write about. Technical writers draft directions for assembling stereo systems, wiring electrical switches, or putting together a dresser or a television stand. Financial officers translate spreadsheets of numbers into reports that explain complicated budgets to boards of directors and shareholders.

All of these real-life writing assignments can be replicated in some manner for authentic writing in school and still permit student choices. For example, students, whether or not they are in journalism classes, can develop news articles and editorials for a classroom bulletin, the school newspaper, or the school's public address announcements or for the school's radio, television, or online student news services. Science and technology students can describe experiments and write directions for completing projects: from how to grow a bean sprout in second grade to how to build a stepstool in middle school. Students in mathematics can translate equations and computations into written descriptions.

The point is that teachers can make school writing more authentic, more like intentional adult writing, by considering assignments and contexts. In general, the more authentic school writing is, the more motivating it is likely to be, especially for students who are struggling to learn how to write well.

MULTIDIMENSIONAL AUTHENTIC RESPONSE WRITING

Motivation plays a key role in helping visual, auditory, and kinesthetic learners become sufficiently interested in written expression to develop the skills needed to write well. Consider a fairly typical example from a high school English class. The class has read Shakespeare's *Romeo and Juliet*. The teacher's goal is to increase students' understanding by having them write about various aspects of the play. Teachers typically approach this instructional task by assigning a series of specific questions for the students to answer. Most textbooks provide such questions. The teacher's goal is to help students tease out new understandings as they search for the answers. Because the teacher already knows the answers, what is considered important has been predetermined for the students. The teacher is merely interested in assessing whether the students also can learn (or can find) the important information.

In a typical school-writing assignment the limits are established by the teacher who is saying to students, in effect, "I know the answers. Do you?" A minimal prompt requiring a minimal response and predetermined criteria for success or failure.

The instructional goal here is really quite limited and, to use the terms from Chapter 1, is virtually guaranteed to require a deliberate, linear response. Natural writers do quite well with this type of assignment. But students who gravitate toward creative thinking may have trouble with it in a couple of ways. They may simply find this preset, find-the-answer-I-already-know approach uninteresting and therefore unmotivating. Or they may search for ways to introduce creativity that sabotage the teacher's intent. Creative students usually are the ones who overthink answers, who drive teachers crazy because they can come up with legitimate-sounding reasons that every choice of a multiple-choice response could be correct.

One way to increase the value of writing in response to reading is to structure prompts that allow all students, regardless of learning style, to choose the topic and the method of the written response. Teachers who do this are using multidimensional instruction that reflects their understanding that differentiated instruction positively affects the construction of knowledge. For example, the teacher might ask students to choose from a smorgasbord of response prompts after reading *Romeo and Juliet:*

- Respond as a drama critic might. What are the strong points of the plot? What are its weaknesses?
- Respond as an editor might by choosing a scene and revising it in some way.
- Respond as a poet might. What images or feelings does the play evoke that give rise to Shakespeare's poetry?
- Respond as a journalist might, as if the play were an account of real events. How could the play, or selected scenes within the play, be reported in a news story or editorial?

The instruction to respond as a _____ might superimposes an authentic role onto an assignment that might otherwise result merely in school writing. Students are given options for responding in ways that suit their interests. The examples in this list, however, are typically linguistic. The roles are all writers': drama critic, editor, poet, and journalist. They are good examples of how creativity can be introduced into what are essentially nonfiction responses to literature. But what about writing prompts for visual, auditory, and kinesthetic learners?

Staying with *Romeo and Juliet*, the following are some response options that will require students to think about the play in nonlinguistic ways and then to reflect their thoughts in writing:

- Respond as a set designer might and describe how you would design the stage setting in order to convey the mood of a particular act or scene.
- Respond as a composer might. Choose a musical form or stylistic time period from the twentieth century (such as Dixieland jazz or '50s rock and roll) and suggest music that could be used to establish moods and settings for a modern-dress production of the play.
- Respond as a choreographer might. What attributes of their characters should the audience be able to see during the sword fight between Mercutio and Tybalt? How should the actors move in order to convey these attributes?

These three prompts ask students to respond, respectively, in terms of visual, auditory, and kinesthetic modes of thought. As a visual artist, the set designer would respond with a drawing; the writing must therefore describe that. In fact, the student might begin by sketching the stage setting and then describe it in words. The composer draws on musical intelligence, and so the student will need to think musically about tones, rhythms, and specific pieces of music first, and then write down those ideas. As a movement specialist, the choreographer would think in steps, gestures, postures, and rhythmic body movement. The kinesthetically inclined student may need to try out steps or work with a partner to discover how the sword fight might be staged to display the characteristics of the roles and then write a description of those characteristics and movements.

AND THEN: **THE PROCESS PHASE**

Instructions to respond as a _____ might following a reading of *Romeo and Juliet* serve as stimuli. The process phase of writing begins with *and then*, more or less. In fact, process often comes into play long before the actual writing of the final work, the ultimate product. Keep in mind the recycling arrow model in Figures 1.1 and 1.2.

The real heart of writing is what happens between the stimulus and the product. The process, in other words. And remember, process is mental and physical, thinking and doing. It makes sense to consider these dimensions both separately and together. But to sort things out, let us examine process from three perspectives: (a) consciousness, (b) speed and elaboration, and (c) mental/physical interaction.

Consciousness

When thinking about thinking, I find it useful to turn to Graham Wallas's *The Art of Thought* (1926), which provides a framework for thinking processes that still is relevant nearly eight decades later. Wallas describes thinking as four sequential stages that are helpful in understanding the writing process:

1. *Preparation* is the stage during which the writer gathers ideas and information and makes a plan. To respond as a _____ might the student must consider the *Romeo and Juliet* text. What information will be needed to frame a response? What are the important ideas? Simply answering these questions may produce an initial, intermediate product such as notes or copies of pertinent dialogue. The writer also will formulate a plan of attack by deciding how to write about the topic and setting limits for the writing project.

2. *Incubation* is the term Wallas uses for the stage during which the writer suspends the conscious mental process but allows it to continue at the subconscious level. The more complex the writing task, the more valuable this rest stage is. Incubation is at work when someone is faced with a tough problem and decides to sleep on it before making a decision. Many students benefit from opportunities to sleep on it when they need to respond to a prompt designed to elicit a complex or thoughtful response. Call it planting a seed or priming the pump, after which incubation often brings order to preparatory data that have been consciously stored during the preparation stage.

3. *Illumination* is the emergence from incubation. The phrase often used is *seeing the light*. The appearance of a happy idea or a sudden inspiration is illumination. Zen Buddhists call this sudden enlightenment *satori*, but it also works for the mundane. Remembering the next morning the name of an author that was frustratingly just on the tip of your tongue yesterday or suddenly recalling where you left your car keys after you had stopped consciously thinking about them—these, too, are examples of illumination following a period of incubation. The organization that comes to consciousness out of the subconscious stage propels the final Wallas stage, verification.

4. *Verification* occurs when the writer moves back to the physical dimension. Verification requires trying out the idea. For the visual learner,

verification may mean drafting in some mnemonic, notational, or textual form: a graphic organizer or a word map. For the auditory learner, verification may involve talking to someone or recording an audiotape. And for the kinesthetic learner, it may mean acting out or walking through the idea. Whatever form this product takes, unless it is the final form, it becomes the stimulus, or preparation, for the next process cycle.

Speed and Elaboration

The rates at which writers pass through Wallas's four stages, the extent of elaboration within the stages, and the number of cycles needed to move from initial stimulus to final product vary greatly. William Zinsser (2001) aptly captures the diversity of writers' approaches to writing in the opening pages of his classic *On Writing Well:*

> There are all kinds of writers and all kinds of methods, and any method that helps you to say what you want to say is the right method for you. Some people write by day, others by night. Some people need silence, others turn on the radio. Some write by hand, some by word processor, some by talking into a tape recorder. Some people write their first draft in one long burst and then revise; others can't write the second paragraph until they have fiddled endlessly with the first. (p. 5)

Some years ago, writer and critic William F. Buckley, Jr., was taken to task for writing too quickly, to which he pointedly responded: "There is no necessary correlation between profundity of thought and the length of time spent on thought" (1986, p. 3). He proceeded to recount how the British author Anthony Trollope imposed a personal goal of writing 250 words every 15 minutes in order to reach his daily quota of 3,500. By contrast, Erle Stanley Gardner, the author of the Perry Mason mysteries and countless other books under a variety of pseudonyms, dictated nonstop to a staff of secretaries.

Mental/Physical Interaction

Speed and elaboration are related to how a writer takes what is in his or her head and gets it onto a page or a computer screen. Interactions between the mental and physical dimensions of the process phase also help to establish a writer's individuality. Benjamin Bloom (1986) uses the term *automaticity* to characterize an interaction marked by the mastery of a physical skill to such a level that a writer, for example, can use the skill with speed and accuracy without giving it conscious thought.

The youngest writers in school can be helped to write more successfully if some support is given to them before they have developed physical automaticity. Being able to talk into a tape recorder, dictate to a classroom aide, or use a voice-activated word-processing program can be valuable for students whose physical writing or keyboarding skills are undeveloped or underdeveloped, including students with disabilities.

When writers are able, for example, to pour out their thoughts virtually nonstop, either writing by hand or using a computer keyboard—or, as in Trollope's case, using a quill pen and ink—they are exhibiting automaticity.

When writers combine automaticity with clarity of thought (or *fluency*), they often can produce consistently publishable prose and a great deal of it. American scientist and science fiction writer Isaac Asimov, French novelist Georges Simenon, and other writers whose total output of books numbered in the hundreds usually report that they revise their writing only slightly before considering it final.

Walter B. Gibson (aka Maxwell Grant, author of *The Shadow* novels) published his first work in 1905, when he was seven years old. By the time he died at age 88, he had written more than a million words a year for much of his career. As his friend, William V. Rauscher, recalls:

> Walter B. Gibson became the ideal example of a professional writer. . . . Creating fiction, nonfiction, almost any subject, posed a challenge for him, and he met each challenge with the same enthusiasm. Perhaps it might be a hardback book, or a booklet which detailed the lives of the presidents. It might be a book on Yoga, or How to Tie Knots, or Hypnotism Through the Ages. The range and breadth of subject matter which he tackled was vast, and his research retention ability was awesome. (http://www.mysticlight press.com/index.php?page_id=131)

For Gibson, the typewriter was an extension of his brain. As Rauscher remembers:

> All the various rooms in Walter's home contained a typewriter. In some of those typewriters, pages of uncompleted articles or projects remained even at the time of his death. With so many typewriters in simultaneous operation, he could work upstairs or downstairs, and shift from one subject to another.

On the other hand, in an earlier era, Henry James found the typewriter something of a nuisance because it altered his mobility. Instead of being able to write when and where inspiration or inclination struck, using nothing more than pen and paper, James found himself confined to his study in order to dictate to a typist whose work schedule did not necessarily coincide with the time when the muse was abroad. Perhaps if James had not been wealthy and had been forced to learn to type for himself, as Gibson had been, he might have felt otherwise.

Ernest Hemingway reportedly combined the tools of physical expression, pen and ink and typewriter. He reputedly wrote the terse dialogue in his novels standing at a typewriter, which he perched on a convenient dresser. But when it came to the descriptive passages, he preferred to sit at a desk and write them in ink.

Hemingway, incidentally, is not the only writer to prefer standing up, at least at times, to write. Indeed, "standing desks" have often been popular. Winston Churchill, who wrote novels and lengthy histories when he was not in government (and sometimes when he was), often stood at such a desk when he wrote.

Mental and physical dimensions are reciprocal. Each instructs the other. There are subtle differences in the way writing is accomplished when drafting is done with a pen or pencil compared to sitting at a keyboard. Dictating to a person differs from dictating to a machine. A person can respond and interact; a machine is mute.

As students mature as writers, they should be encouraged to find their own best ways to write. (Note: It's *ways*, plural.) Certain subjects and forms of writing may be best handled differently. The writing teacher's job is to help students build a personal repertoire of successful writing strategies, not to find the one best way. It doesn't exist.

PATHWAYS TO FLUENCY

Automaticity in the preceding discussion has been circumscribed by a physical skill, such as keyboarding prowess. Its mental counterpart is *fluency*. Writers like those described above are prolific because they are fluent. That is, they construct ideas mentally that are more fully developed than those created by writers who must resort to some form of physical development or planning, such as making an outline or rehearsing. Buckley, Gibson, Simenon, Asimov, and others wrote fast, as Buckley did, by opening the floodgates of the mind and allowing the ideas, the essays, the stories, to pour onto the page fully formed.

Fluency is a concept that is central to teaching visual, auditory, and kinesthetic writers to write well. Physical automaticity and the ability to form ideas into words in one's mind must at some point merge. After all, there is little reason to attain great proficiency at keyboarding if the writer is going to sit, fingers poised above the keys, staring at the screen with nothing to say; or, rather, with his or her ideas bound up in a mental tangle that cannot be undone without resorting to some intermediate step.

For linguistic-logical learners, the road to fluency can be relatively straight. Teachers can employ a number of instructional strategies to help these students build a capacity to write quickly and confidently, such as using fluency journals and giving students fluency practice using writing prompts with timed responses. But the road will have some hills and curves for visual, auditory, and kinesthetic learners because these learners are less likely to think in words until they have first formed ideas as images, sounds, and movements. Understanding this characteristic is an important starting point. Rather than leaping to linguistic-logical strategies for developing fluency, teachers who want their visual, auditory, and kinesthetic learners to develop fluency must begin by helping students develop fluency in using images, sounds, and movements.

Once visual, auditory, and kinesthetic learners develop proficiency using their preferred learning styles, they will be better able to internalize those processes—that is, to think and plan using mental images, sounds, and movements. When they reach a stage of internal fluency, these students can work on developing the linguistic-logical proficiency that will allow them to put words to their mental constructions and pour those words onto paper. As they learn how to externalize this mental prewriting, they will be able to write quickly, confidently, and thoroughly in situations (such as writing an essay on a standardized test) in which extensive external prewriting and planning are not permitted.

Linguistic-logical learners can develop adequate fluency through direct instruction, but exposure to visual, auditory, and kinesthetic strategies can be helpful to these students too, because these learners also will increase their repertoire of successful writing strategies.

SAMPLE LESSON 2.1: RESPOND AS A _____ MIGHT

To pull together this chapter's themes of authenticity, multidimensional responding, and process phase, a sample lesson will be useful. This lesson uses the framework introduced earlier (respond as a _____ might) and can serve as a model that can be adapted for students of various ages. In this case, students are asked to respond as a camp leader might.

Why a camp leader? Well, why not? Camping in some form is a common pastime both as a family and as a youth-group activity. Many schools include a camping experience as part of the environmental studies curriculum in upper elementary school. Historical accounts of camping figure in fiction and nonfiction, including wilderness camping in the story of the Lewis and Clark expedition or in Jack London's story "To Build a Fire" (although the latter might discourage anyone from camping, at least in the winter).

The objective of this lesson is to make visible one or more planning (or prewriting) activities and then to write. Students who already have developed a high degree of fluency may be inclined simply to draft a response in reasonably finished form. They will benefit more from this lesson by exploring a way of planning that they do not customarily use. Visual, auditory, and kinesthetic learners can choose a planning strategy suited to their preferred learning style, but they also may want to explore other strategies in order to increase their repertoire of planning strategies.

Background: Students have read about camping—in a history lesson, a short story, or in the context of preparing for a real camping experience—and have discussed aspects of camping, such as where to go, what to pack, and what activities to plan for. Teachers who want to expand on this lesson might want to consider using one of the book resources below.

Assignment choices: Students should choose one of the following assignments and may work alone or with a partner:

• Design a campsite layout. There will be six campers using three tents. What setting will work best for the campsite? What elements must be included, such as tents, a campfire, safe equipment storage, and so forth? Draw the layout and then write a description. (Visual)

• Create a key to birdsongs or calls. When it is quiet in the woods, campers can hear the songs or calls of various birds even though they may not be able to see the birds. Research the songs or calls of five birds likely to be heard in the campground. Try to imitate the sounds and then write a description. (Auditory)

• Roll and store a sleeping bag. Each camper will be responsible for rolling and storing his or her own sleeping bag. The bags will be easier to carry if they are rolled and bagged correctly. Experiment with a sleeping bag to discover how best to roll it and then write a description. (Kinesthetic)

Book Resources

Various school texts contain fiction or nonfiction about camping. The following are a few sample trade books that may be useful in expanding this sample lesson:

Hodgson, M. (2000). *Camping for dummies.* Foster City, CA: IDG Books Worldwide. From the popular *For Dummies* series, suitable for high school readers.

O'Bannon, A., & Clelland, M. (2001). *Allen and Mike's really cool backpackin' book: Traveling and camping skills for a wilderness environment.* Helena, MT: Falcon. Humorously illustrated but authoritative guide for middle-level students and older.

Parish, P. (2003). *Amelia Bedelia goes camping.* New York: HarperTrophy. From the popular series for young readers.

Rey, M., & Rey, H. A. (1999). *Curious George goes camping.* Boston: Houghton Mifflin. From the popular series for young readers.

Townsend, C. (2004). *The backpacker's guide* (3rd ed.). Camden, ME: International Marine/Ragged Mountain Press. Well-researched guide for middle school readers and older.

SAMPLE LESSON 2.2: MULTIDIMENSIONAL AUTHENTIC RESPONSE WRITING

Authenticity, multidimensional responding, and process phases are emphasized in this sample lesson. This lesson uses the framework introduced in Chapter 2 (respond as a _____ might) and can be adapted for students of various ages.

This lesson is based on a text that may be chosen by the teacher, by student groups, or by individual students. The selection might be a scene from a short story, a novel, a play, or a nonfiction work of historical or scientific description. The choice should allow visual, auditory, and kinesthetic learners to engage their preferred learning style.

Background: Students have read the chosen text and discussed its descriptive characteristics. For example, the text might be a passage describing the scene at Gettysburg on the day that Lincoln delivered his famous address.

Assignment choices: Students, individually or in small groups, should choose one of the following assignments:

- Respond as a set designer might if this scene were to be included in a Civil War drama. Describe how you would design a stage setting in order to convey the mood of this scene. (Visual)
- Respond as a composer might if asked to choose music to be played on this historic occasion. Rather than research historical music, describe the type of music you would choose and why. What kinds of response would you look for in the audience gathered to hear President Lincoln? (Auditory)
- Respond as an event organizer might. Who will be included in the proceedings (or who were included)? What role should each individual take in this historic event: Who stands where, and who speaks when? (Kinesthetic)

REFERENCES

Bloom, B. (1986). Automaticity. *Educational Leadership*, 44(5), 70–77.

Buckley, W. F., Jr. (1986, February 9). With all deliberate speed: What's so bad about writing fast? *New York Times Book Review*, p. 3.

Rauscher, W. V. (n.d.). *Walter B. Gibson—Wizard of words.* Retrieved November 22, 2004, from http://www.mysticlightpress.com/index.php?page_id=131

Wallas, G. (1926). *The art of thought.* New York: Harcourt, Brace.

Zinsser, W. (2001). *On writing well.* (25th anniversary ed.). New York: Harper Resource.

3 Observing, Then Writing

In Chapter 2 the sample lesson focused on camping. I suggested that students choose one of three assignments or prompts:

- Design a campsite layout. Draw the layout and then write a description. (Visual)
- Create a key to birdsongs or calls. Try to imitate the sounds and then write a description. (Auditory)
- Roll and store a sleeping bag. Experiment with a sleeping bag to discover how best to roll it and then write a description. (Kinesthetic)

Each of these prompts requires the student to make a *translation*—that is, to translate a visual design, birdcalls, or a physical activity (rolling a sleeping bag) into words. For this assignment the translation is a description. For others the required writing might entail explication or analysis. And so the question for this chapter is: How can teachers help students take the result (the product) of their prewriting or planning process and, using it as a further stimulus, translate that visual, auditory, or kinesthetic product into a written draft?

SENSORY REPORTAGE

One way to begin working with visual, auditory, and kinesthetic students on translating their planning into drafting is to look closely at the words they use. In this case, because the students have been asked to describe something, the focus will be on descriptive words. Students who are familiar with the traditional parts of speech know that those words are adjectives, verbs,

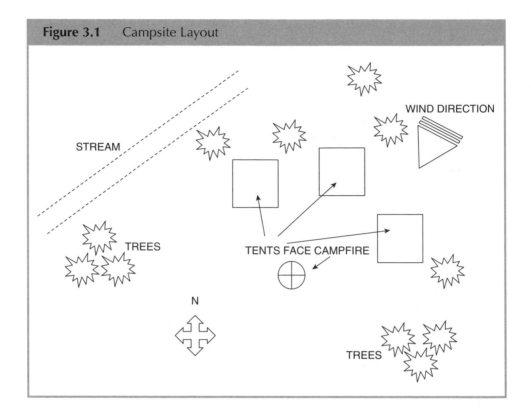

Figure 3.1   Campsite Layout

and adverbs, in roughly that order of importance. Precise nouns will count, and prepositional phrases also will be useful. But, of course, students can use these parts of speech without naming them. Their definitions are sufficient. Adjectives describe people, places, and things. Verbs convey states of existence or actions. Prepositional phrases describe relationships. And so on.

It is important for students to realize that translating from a visual, auditory, or kinesthetic plan will entail an intermediate prewriting process. A student gathering the words that will be used to write the draft can be compared to a chef preparing to cook. Having decided on a meal, the chef must gather the ingredients before preparing the dishes.

The translation involved in moving from a visual, auditory, or kines-thetic plan to a written draft can be thought of as *sensory reportage*. The reporter must gather the facts and then assemble them into a story, much as the chef assembles ingredients and then cooks the meal. The key ques-tion is this: What words describe the sensory experiences?

Let us assume that Figure 3.1 is a design made in response to the first prompt above. It shows a campsite with a nearby stream, various trees, three tents, and a campfire. The layout sketch shows the geography of the camp-site with directional keys, and it also shows the prevailing wind direction.

VISUAL REPORTAGE

A starting point for students will be to brainstorm a list of words or phrases to draw from as they draft their descriptions. Choosing these words is important because the goal of descriptive writing is to create prose that allows the reader to imagine, to feel the sensations felt by the writer. Individual students can do this on their own, but brainstorming can be more effective if the students work in pairs, triads, or small groups. With what words might the campsite in Figure 3.1 be described? Following is a short list of possible words and phrases:

- clean water source
- nearby stream
- open space/clearing
- wind from the northeast
- tents face away from the wind
- tents face the campfire and shelter the campfire from the wind
- trees shelter the tents but don't hang over the campfire

This list becomes another product/stimulus. The sensory reportage in this case involves taking the first product, the campsite layout, translating it into a second product, a list of words and phrases, and then translating the list into prose. Here's how the student might write the description:

> The campsite has a source of clean water, a nearby stream. The wind blows mainly from the northeast, and so the tents are set up to face away from the wind. The tents face the campfire and shelter it from the wind. The clearing is large enough so that tree branches don't hang over the campfire but give some shelter to the tents.

This is an example of straightforward, third-person (observer) description. The student describes the campsite by stating what goes where and why. Because the planning product is visual, the description is largely in visual terms. Later, we will discuss taking this foundation and building in two directions: translating from one type of writing to another, such as from third-person description to first-person narrative, and developing multisensory descriptions. Sensory reportage in this context is limited to the sensory basis, whether visual, auditory, or kinesthetic.

AUDITORY REPORTAGE

Students might brainstorm a different kind of written list when responding to the prompt that calls for a key to the birdsongs or calls that campers are likely to hear. For example:

Bobwhite: a two-tone, short-long call; sounds like the bird is saying its name

Screech owl: a sharp call (screech) followed by a long *oo*

Pileated woodpecker: a choppy call like a burst of bird laughter— *ha-ha-ha-ha-ha*; also the knocking noise as the bird "sounds," or pecks, on trees

Chickadee: a short, faint, high-pitched sort of *see-saw*

Crow: a short, repeated *caw*

The resulting description might read as follows:

Campers may hear many birds that they can't see, because either the birds are hidden in trees during the day or can't be seen at night. The bobwhite makes a two-tone call, a short tone followed by a longer one, as if the bird is saying its name, *bob-whiiite*. The screech-owl is well named because it screeches, making a sharp noise that is followed by a long *oo*. The call of the pileated wood-pecker sounds like choppy laughter, *ha-ha-ha-ha-ha*. Woodpeckers also "sound," or peck on trees, making a rapid knocking noise. Chickadees call using a short, light-sounding *see-saw* tone. The crow makes a loud, repeated *caw*.

This example of descriptive writing concentrates on the auditory, using descriptive words and phrases—a two-tone call, screeches, choppy laughter—and imitative language—*bob-whiiite*, *ha-ha-ha-ha-ha*, *see-saw*. Because most students are less adept at auditory than visual description, this can be a good opportunity to encourage students to use additional resources such as recordings of birdcalls and Web sites that will play short samples of birdsongs and calls. (One for Florida birds for example, can be found at www.flmnh.ufl.edu/natsci/ornithology/sounds.htm.) Students can listen to the calls several times as they decide how to describe them.

Another resource is a thesaurus, as either a book or an electronic pro-gram. While pronunciations and imitative language will not be searchable, some descriptive words will be. For example, the following synonyms can be found for *screech:*

- hoot
- shriek
- squawk
- scream

- shrill
- squeal
- yell

Several process activities are needed to move students from imitating the actual birdcalls to finding descriptive words and phrases and then to a draft of a text that incorporates those words and phrases.

KINESTHETIC REPORTAGE

The third prompt can be acted out with a real sleeping bag or an imaginary one. While it is a good idea to use the real thing, especially with younger students, the goal is that the student be able to visualize actions. After all, if the prompt on a test is to describe how to roll a sleeping bag, the student will not have an opportunity for real hands-on processing but will need to think kinesthetically.

One way to prepare students for kinesthetic reportage is to ask them to work in pairs, one student performing the action (or miming it) and the other recording what is being done. Many actions, such as rolling a sleeping bag, are sequential, and so this also is a good time to attend to words that indicate order, such as *first, second, next, then,* and *finally.* As students brainstorm, the natural product may be a numbered list showing sequence. For example:

1. Lay the sleeping bag out flat.

2. Zip the bag closed.

3. Roll the bag, starting from the closed end.

4. Keep the roll tight.

5. Sit on the roll to keep it together while you put one end into the stuff sack.

6. Stuff the sleeping bag into the sack, pulling the drawstring tight.

The description of the action might then read this way:

To roll and store a sleeping bag, the camper starts by laying the bag flat and zipping it closed. Then the camper rolls the bag, beginning at the closed end. The roll should be tight. When the bag is rolled up, the camper sits on the roll to keep it from unrolling and slips the stuff sack over one end of the roll. Finally, the camper stuffs the sleeping bag into the sack and pulls the drawstring tight to close the sack.

A couple of variations on this activity-based brainstorming are also useful. One calls for the student who is acting out to do so silently while the observing student records what she or he sees. The observer can say what the steps are while recording them: "I see you are laying out the sleeping bag and zipping it up. Now you are starting to roll from the closed end. You are keeping the roll very tight," and so on. If the observer gets it wrong, the performer can offer a correction.

Another variation is to ask the student who is doing the action to say what he or she is doing while doing it so that the observer can record what is said: "I am laying out the bag and then zipping it shut. Now I'm moving to the closed end and starting to roll it up tightly. . . ."

Both variations help students generate the words that suit the actions through the interaction of movement and speech. The list becomes the next product/stimulus and gets translated into a draft text.

TRANSLATION INTO DIFFERENT FORMS

The preceding visual, auditory, and kinesthetic exercises can be extended to help students become adept at translating their drafts into various points of view. For example, the draft about the campsite layout is a third-person description:

> *The campsite* has a source of clean water, a nearby stream. The wind blows mainly from the northeast, and so *the tents are set up* to face away from the wind. The tents face the campfire and shelter it from the wind. *The clearing is* large enough so that tree branches don't hang over *the campfire* but give some shelter to *the tents*.

Teachers can point out the features of this draft that indicate the point of view, such as the use of the observer's perspective, illustrated by the italics. "What if," the teacher might then ask, "you put yourself into this scene? How might the underlined words be changed to include a first-person observer?" Teacher and students might then work together, using chart paper or an overhead or LCD projector, to make the following changes:

> *Our campsite* has a source of clean water, a nearby stream. The wind blows mainly from the northeast, and so *we set up our tents* to face away from the wind. The tents face the campfire and shelter it from

the wind. *We found a clearing* large enough so that tree branches don't hang over *our campfire* but give some shelter to *our tents.*

Teaching students how to translate their planning into different points of view helps develop fluency because the students are encouraged to use the same plan in various ways, which helps to convey the notion that the plan itself is fluid. Making translation visible as a class exercise can be more effective than working one-on-one with students, which is very time-consuming, or asking them simply to work on their own.

"Instead of merely describing the campsite, let's assume that the lay-out is an ideal," the teacher might go on to say. "How would you rephrase the description as exposition—that is, as a set of directions to be given directly to another person?" Again, teacher and students might work together to come up with something like this:

> *Choose a* campsite *that* has a source of clean water, *such as* a nearby stream. *If* the wind blows mainly from the northeast, *as shown in the diagram, then set up* ~~and so~~ the tents ~~are set up~~ to face away from the wind. The tents *should* face the campfire and shelter it from the wind. The clearing *should be* large enough so that tree branches don't hang over the campfire but give some shelter to the tents.

Teachers should point out that directions, as in this example, often use an implied, second-person viewpoint. What the student really is writing is: "*You* choose a campsite. . . ."

By using these three translations, the teacher has introduced students to first-, second-, and third-person approaches to the same information— all from a single planning activity. This approach can be replicated for the auditory and kinesthetic exercises as well. Using whole-class instruction for this type of lesson allows students to add this approach to their reper-toire of learning-style preferences.

Translation used in this way also introduces the concept of editing not as correction but as a means of changing a text to suit various purposes. (Editing will be taken up in greater detail in later chapters.)

SENSE EXPLORATION

To this point the focus has been on students using the learning style they prefer or exploring an alternative style that concentrates on one sense. The visual prompt called for a visual-spatial response, the auditory for a sound response, the kinesthetic for a movement response. At some point, usually

Figure 3.2   Sense Exploration Template

Sight	Hearing	Smell	Touch	Taste

after students have gained at least some experience with single-sense reportage, it is important to introduce multisensory responding. One way to teach this is through *sense exploration*—a term and strategy I began using some time ago and have found very useful (Walling, 1974, 1978, 1979).

One way to introduce sense exploration is with a simple assignment, the response to which will be the *before* description. The initial assignment I have typically used is this: *Describe this classroom.* Students are allowed time to plan in whatever manner they choose, and then write. Following is a characteristic response:

> Our classroom is a rectangular room with tan walls. There are three chalkboards and two bulletin boards. The teacher's desk is just inside the door. There are 34 student desks, but two are not used. The students are all sitting and writing this assignment. The teacher is walking around the room.

After the students have written their drafts, I ask them to share with one another so that they can get a feel for what some of their classmates have written. Then I show the students Figure 3.2 and ask them to analyze their drafts by identifying the sensory perceptions—expressed as descriptive words—they used and recording them in the appropriate column. Almost without exception, their responses will fall predominantly in the sight column.

We live in a visual culture, so naturally we rely on visual perception to inform our writing—unless we make an effort to include other sensory input. Even auditory and kinesthetic learners fall into this visually dominant

Figure 3.3   Classroom Description—Sense Exploration Template

Sight	Hearing	Smell	Touch	Taste
Rectangular room Tan walls 3 chalkboards 2 bulletin boards Teacher's desk near door 34 student desks—2 not used Students writing Teacher walking around	Teacher's footsteps Pencils scratching on paper Someone closing a locker in the hall Feet shuffling under desks	Mary's lemony cologne My bubble gum breath	Smooth paper Fingers gripping the pencil hard Pebbly walls Dense carpet	Stale gum Pizza with pepperoni

way of thinking and perceiving until they are prodded to consider other types of sensory input.

The next step is to ask students to set aside the before draft and to use their analysis chart as a planning device. The goal is to note other types of sensory input, then record their impressions in the appropriate columns. Figure 3.3 is an example of a sense exploration chart that has been fleshed out in this way.

Once the planning chart has been completed, the students are ready to create a new draft. When they have finished writing, they will share their work again. It will become clear to everyone that the new *after* drafts are longer and richer in detail. They more completely and accurately describe the classroom. Here's an example:

> Our classroom is a rectangular, carpeted room with pebbly tan walls. There are three chalkboards and two bulletin boards. There are 34 student desks, but two are not used. The teacher's desk is just inside the door, but the teacher is walking around while we write. I hear her footsteps and the sound of students' feet shuffling under desks as our pencils scratch across smooth paper. Someone in the hall is closing a locker. My fingers are gripping the pencil hard as I try to think of what to write. Mary's lemony cologne is distracting me. My bubble gum is getting stale. I probably have bubble gum breath. I'm looking forward to the taste of pizza with pepperoni for lunch next period.

Even more than the camping prompt, the classroom description draws on students' firsthand experiences—some students may have experienced camping only through reading. The point of this is to keep early developmental writing experiences grounded in students' realities. Descriptive writing is a good example of observing, then writing. And it requires less formal research, more complex thought, and greater planning.

WRITING UP THE TAXONOMY

Remembering Bloom's taxonomy can be helpful as a framework for guiding student writing practice. Why Bloom's taxonomy? It's familiar. It's simple. And it's useful. Bloom (1956) proposed that intellectual activity could be thought of in terms of six successively more complex categories of operation:

1. *Knowledge*: storing information or recalling data. Key words include *arrange, define, label, list, memorize, name,* and *repeat.*

2. *Comprehension*: understanding and translating information. Key words include *classify, describe, discuss, explain, express, identify,* and *restate.*

3. *Application*: using information in a new context. Key words include *apply, demonstrate, illustrate,* and *interpret.*

4. *Analysis*: separating concepts into component parts so that the structure or organization can be understood. Key words include *analyze, appraise, calculate, categorize, compare, contrast, criticize,* and *distinguish.*

5. *Synthesis*: building a whole from diverse parts to create a new structure or meaning. Key words include *assemble, collect, compose, construct, design,* and *develop.*

6. *Evaluation*: making judgments about meaning, validity, and so on. Key words include *appraise, assess, defend, judge,* and *predict.*

Bloom's taxonomy sometimes is represented as a pyramid, as in Figure 3.4. The idea is to help students write up the pyramid—that is, to gain proficiency at increasingly more complex writing processes.

Much of the writing students are asked to do involves merely demonstrating knowledge. Teachers ask students to recall information that they have read or heard and to repeat it. Bloom's taxonomy can be used by teachers as a rubric for planning writing lessons. Recalling and reporting are basic translations: starting points, if you will, but just that. If students are to learn how to write well, they must learn to think with greater complexity and then to make their complex thinking transparent in writing.

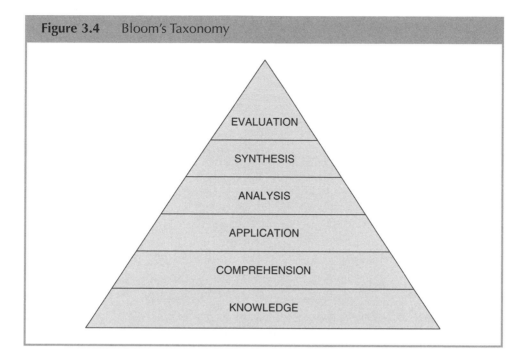

Figure 3.4   Bloom's Taxonomy

EVALUATION

SYNTHESIS

ANALYSIS

APPLICATION

COMPREHENSION

KNOWLEDGE

There's an old saw in journalism that the best writers do not write to be understood, they write not to be misunderstood.

Recalling and reporting are bases from which to work toward greater cognitive sophistication. The descriptive writing required in the examples in this chapter and the previous one moves students up the pyramid a step, to the comprehension level. As succeeding chapters unfold, it will help to be mindful of Bloom's taxonomy and the notion that helping visual, auditory, and kinesthetic students learn to write well can be best accomplished by structuring lessons so that they require increasing sophistication. Writing instruction should not leap from base to peak but should ask students to take successive steps up the pyramid. For some students, using their preferred learning style to move from sensory to multisensory reportage (as illustrated in the sense exploration exercise) can be a challenging step, because sense exploration followed by writing verges on application, Bloom's third level up the pyramid.

SAMPLE LESSON 3.1: TEMPLATE AND CHECKLIST STRATEGIES

In keeping with the idea of writing from authentic observation, the following prompt and procedures illustrate another way to approach a descriptive-writing exercise.

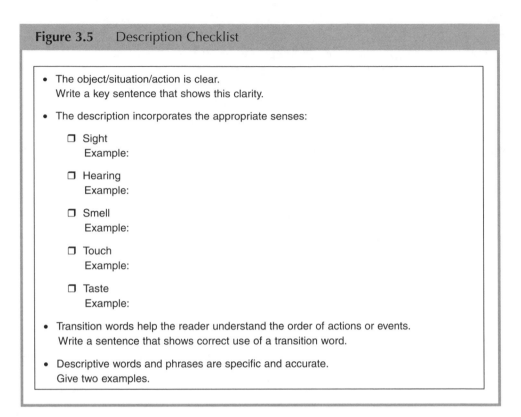

Figure 3.5 Description Checklist

- The object/situation/action is clear.
  Write a key sentence that shows this clarity.

- The description incorporates the appropriate senses:

  ☐ Sight
     Example:

  ☐ Hearing
     Example:

  ☐ Smell
     Example:

  ☐ Touch
     Example:

  ☐ Taste
     Example:

- Transition words help the reader understand the order of actions or events.
  Write a sentence that shows correct use of a transition word.

- Descriptive words and phrases are specific and accurate.
  Give two examples.

Copyright © 2006 by Corwin Press. All rights reserved. Reprinted from *Teaching Writing to Visual, Auditory, and Kinesthetic Learners*, by Donovan R. Walling. Thousand Oaks, CA: Corwin Press, www .corwinpress.com. Reproduction authorized only for the local school site or nonprofit organization that has purchased this book.

Background: A number of careers require workers to observe something and then write a description of what they observed. Quality-control and time-management professionals examine factory operations, for example. Scientists observe birds and animals. Traffic controllers regulate the movements of land or air vehicles. The ability to make careful observations and then set them down in writing is a valuable skill.

Assignment: Students will work in pairs to take up an observation post somewhere in or near the school: at an entrance, the cafeteria or gymnasium, the school bus pickup point, on a busy stairway landing, or somewhere else students are likely to be moving about. The paired observers each will record their observations over a five-minute period. Each student will use a sense exploration template (Figure 3.2) as the record-keeping tool. After the observation period, the two students will compare notes and then work together to draft a description.

Description checklist: In addition to the sense exploration template, teachers can now introduce students to a description checklist (Figure 3.5) that can be used in several ways. Before the observation, students can review the checklist so that they better understand what is expected from their draft. Following the observation and note-taking, as students plan their composition, they can use the checklist again (along with the sense exploration template) to ensure that all of the expected elements will be present in their draft. Finally, after writing, the checklist can be used for self-assessment or to guide the review of other students' drafts.

Why a template and a checklist? In moving students toward greater sophistication in thinking and writing, teachers need to expose them to new ways of examining what they do and how they do it. The sense exploration template provides a way to record sensory impressions, to gather descriptive words. This template can be used to help students with a variety of assignments because most writing is descriptive. In this sample assignment, the template serves as a note-taking form.

The description checklist asks students to attend to more than sense description. It incorporates the idea (without labeling it as such) of a topic sentence, and students are asked to think about transition words. The checklist also asks students to analyze the draft by citing examples from the text that they or their classmates have written so that it moves students up the pyramid to Bloom's fourth level: analysis.

SAMPLE LESSON 3.2: OBSERVATION AND SENSORY REPORTAGE

Writing from authentic observation is an important nonfiction writing skill. The following prompt and procedures incorporate sensory reportage to stimulate thorough observation—but with a twist.

Background: The ability to make careful observations and set them down in writing is a valuable skill. However, too often we only report what is visible because vision is the dominant sense for most humans. To focus on the other senses, this assignment eliminates the visual.

Assignment: Use the following steps in telling students what you would have them do:

1. Explain that students will be writing directions to be read to a blind visitor to the school. The visitor must walk unassisted from point A to point B (for example, from the front door of the school to the door of the classroom).

2. Allow students to work individually or in pairs to discover the nonvisual features of the route. One student may choose to lead another student who is blindfolded, for example. Or a student may explore the route independently. Ask students to catalog sounds, textures (wall, floor), turns, stairs, and so forth that they encounter. Ask students to record their observations on a sense exploration template (Figure 3.2) with the sight column omitted and to add directional indicators (left, right, up, down).

3. After their observation, ask students to write their directions, paying attention to their catalog of features. Stress also the need to use effective sequence words, such as *first, second, then,* and *next.*

4. Direct students to exchange papers, so that they can try out one another's directions and give constructive feedback to the writer.

5. Ask students to revise their directions based on the feedback they receive.

This lesson should be spread over two or three days so that each step can be completed in a meaningful way.

REFERENCES

Bloom, B. S. (Ed.). (1956). *Taxonomy of educational objective: Vol. 1. The cognitive domain.* New York: McKay.

Walling, D. R. (1974). Sense exploration into media: An introduction. *Audiovisual Instruction, 19*(8), 13–15.

Walling, D. R. (1978, Fall). Sense exploration and descriptive writing. *Exercise exchange.* Burlington: University of Vermont, English department publication.

Walling, D. R. (1979). Creating mood through diction. *English Journal, 68*(4), 71.

4 Organizing Artistically

E xamples in the preceding chapters have focused on short pieces of writing, usually only one paragraph. And so far the only organizing device touched on has been the use of transition words when giving directions. The focus of this chapter is *artistic organization*—the use of visual, auditory, and kinesthetic learning styles, the so-called artistic learning styles. Although they are best suited to these learning styles, such organizational strategies can also be used by linear-logical learners to enlarge their repertoire of thinking and writing strategies.

PEARLS-ON-A-STRING ORGANIZATION

Directions can be thought of as a series of ideas that are connected in a sequence, like pearls on a string. To give directions, the writer begins with the first idea, then goes on to the next and the next until the end is reached. When this type of writing is planned using a graphic organizer (or idea map, to use another familiar term), the graphic looks like a string of pearls (see Figure 4.1).

The directions for locating a campsite in Chapter 3 read as follows:

Choose a campsite that has a source of clean water, such as a nearby stream. If the wind blows mainly from the northeast, as shown in the diagram, then set up the tents to face away from the wind. The tents should face the campfire and shelter it from the wind. The clearing should be large enough so that tree branches don't hang over the campfire but give some shelter to the tents.

This paragraph might be represented graphically as shown in Figure 4.2.

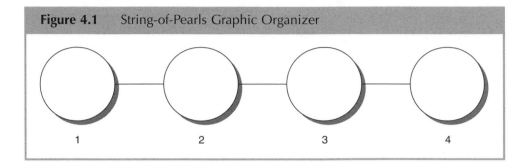

Figure 4.1   String-of-Pearls Graphic Organizer

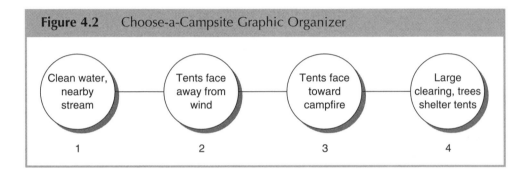

Figure 4.2   Choose-a-Campsite Graphic Organizer

Representing pearls on a string, this visual device is intended to be a graphic organizer. When teaching about paragraphs or longer texts that depend on a strong, driving beginning (the engine), supporting details (the cars), and a specific conclusion (the caboose), teachers may find a train to be another useful metaphor.

An auditory equivalent of pearls on a string is notes on a musical score. When a composer sets down a tune, he or she constructs a line of notes that harmonize with and complement each other. The notes, like a set of directions, follow one after the other in a musically logical order. Auditory learners can be helped if they think of composing a piece of writing as a songwriter might compose a song.

A kinesthetic equivalent of pearls on a string is steps in a dance. When a dancer moves, he or she puts one foot down in a specific way and then puts the other foot down in a specific way, and so on until the dance is complete. What should the first step look like? And the next? And so on.

Organizational metaphors, whether visual, auditory, or kinesthetic, serve as mnemonic devices. Once students internalize these metaphors and can mentally see, hear, or feel them, they will have a mental repertoire of organizational processes to which they can turn whenever they are confronted by a new writing challenge.

Figure 4.3 Pearl Necklace Graphic Organizer

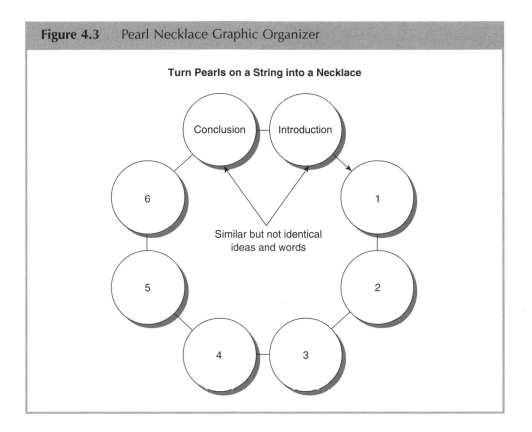

Organizational metaphors such as pearls on a string also can be manipulated and adapted for new purposes. For example, to teach students about writing introductions and conclusions that echo one another the teacher might turn the string of pearls into a necklace, as shown in Figure 4.3.

Following is an example paragraph that might be organized using this type of graphic organizer.

When I really think about our classroom, I am amazed by the way my senses all are touched. Our classroom is a rectangular, carpeted room with pebbly tan walls. There are three chalkboards and two bulletin boards. There are 34 student desks, but two are not used. The teacher's desk is just inside the door, but the teacher is walking around while we write. I hear her footsteps and the sound of students' feet shuffling under desks as our pencils scratch across smooth paper. Someone in the hall is closing a locker. My fingers are gripping the pencil hard as I try to think of what to write. Mary's lemony cologne is distracting me. My bubble gum is getting stale. I probably have bubble gum breath. I'm looking forward to the taste of pizza with pepperoni for lunch next period. *Now I'll think about the lunchroom differently. I wonder how all of my senses will be touched there.*

Readers will recall the main text of this paragraph as one of the examples in Chapter 3. A new beginning and a new ending have been added to complete the description. Notice that the italicized sentences echo the same ideas without using identical wording. If students were assigned the task of making a longer composition, the conclusion also could serve to establish a transition to a next paragraph, which would logically describe the lunchroom.

INDUCTIVE AND DEDUCTIVE ORGANIZATION

Inductive reasoning arrives at a general principle based on particular facts or instances. Deductive reasoning is essentially the opposite—that is, applying a general principle and reasoning to a specific conclusion or set of conclusions. These twin notions of organization can be more simply stated as parts-to-a-whole and whole-to-the-parts reasoning. Figure 4.4 illustrates both of these simply by changing the direction of the arrows.

These are two more graphic organizers that are particularly effective for visual learners, but they can be adapted to match the learning styles of auditory and kinesthetic learners. Other visual, auditory, and kinesthetic metaphors abound:

Visual metaphors

Inductive: Mixing colors, such as putting together red and blue to make purple

Deductive: Identifying the types of trees in a landscape painting or photograph

Auditory metaphors

Inductive: Combining notes played on a musical instrument to make a chord

Deductive: Listening for the types of instruments played or parts sung within a song

Kinesthetic metaphors

Inductive: Putting together puzzle pieces to complete a scene

Deductive: Analyzing each actor's movement in a scene or act of a play

Figure 4.4   Inductive and Deductive Graphic Organizers

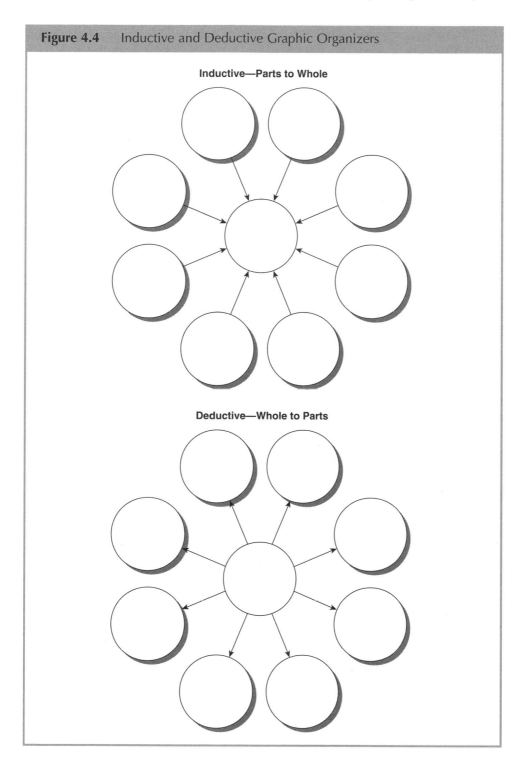

The metaphors are infinitely adaptable. If a kinesthetic learner is more into sports than theater, for example, the deductive metaphor of analyzing

each player's movement in a football scrimmage works as well as the stage metaphor.

The following sample paragraph, which was introduced in Chapter 3, works well as an example for students. The teacher might ask, "Is this paragraph organized inductively or deductively?"

> Campers may hear many birds that they can't see, either because the birds are hidden in trees during the day or can't be seen at night. The bobwhite makes a two-tone call, a short tone followed by a longer one, as if the bird is saying its name, *bob-whiiite*. The screech-owl is well named because it screeches, making a sharp noise that is followed by a long *oo* sound. The call of the pileated woodpecker sounds like choppy laughter, *ha-ha-ha-ha-ha*. Wood-peckers also "sound," or peck on trees, making a rapid knocking noise. Chickadees call using a short, light-sounding *see-saw* tone. The crow makes a loud, repeated *caw*.

With practice, students will be able to identify this paragraph as one using whole-to-parts organization. The writer announces in the first sentence that campers "may hear many birds" without being able to see them—a general statement—and then goes on to describe several specific birds according to the calls they make.

As in the acquisition of any skill, practice here is essential. And so a helpful next step is to ask students to translate, in this case from inductive to deductive. The teacher might say, "Let's remove the first sentence and put the specifics of this paragraph first. What is the general statement of principle that can be drawn from the specifics?" The example might then look something like this:

> Campers should listen carefully. The bobwhite makes a two-tone call, a short tone followed by a longer one, as if the bird is saying its name, *bob-whiiite*. The screech-owl is well named because it screeches, making a sharp noise that is followed by a long *oo* sound. The call of the pileated woodpecker sounds like choppy laughter, *ha-ha-ha-ha-ha*. Woodpeckers also "sound," or peck on trees, making a rapid knocking noise. Chickadees call using a short, light-sounding *see-saw* tone. The crow makes a loud, repeated *caw*. Campers may hear many birds that they can't see, because either the birds are hidden in trees during the day or can't be seen at night. But they can still identify these birds by listening for their distinctive calls.

Students should have many opportunities both to practice various organizing strategies and to translate from one strategy to another. As discussed in Chapter 2, this type of practice with authentic writing helps students internalize the strategies and gain confidence and fluency in their use. I keep drawing on and adapting examples from previous chapters to demonstrate this notion of translation. Teachers can use this strategy to help students see more clearly the similarities and differences that distinguish these writing processes.

INVERTED PYRAMID ORGANIZATION

Journalism, whether print (newspapers, magazines), electronic (Internet), or broadcast (radio, television), relies on a traditional form of organization referred to as the inverted pyramid. The inverted pyramid is a mnemonic for getting the most important information—the news—up front so that the reader who may have time to read or hear only part of the news story will learn the basic facts immediately. Figure 4.5 is an illustration of the inverted pyramid.

At the top, or most important, layer are the journalist's main concerns: who, what, when, where, why, and how. (These often are referred to simply as the five W's and H.) In Chapter 3 the sample lesson assignment asked students to work in pairs and collect information during a five-minute observation. One way to organize that information (or to reorganize it, that is, to translate it into a new organization) is to use this inverted pyramid strategy. For example, if the students took up an observation post near the cafeteria, they could consider how answers to the following questions might be used to lead off their description.

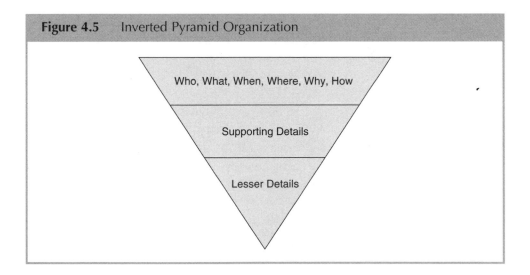

Figure 4.5   Inverted Pyramid Organization

Who, What, When, Where, Why, How

Supporting Details

Lesser Details

Whom did you see entering and leaving the cafeteria?

What were the subjects (students, teachers, cafeteria workers) doing as they came and went?

When did you make your observation?

Where were you standing in relation to the area you observed?

Why did you make the observation?

How did you record what you saw and heard?

What follows is how one student might record the scene, mindful that the directions also asked the students to use their sense exploration template (Figure 3.5):

Terry and I decided to stand in the hallway across from the main door to the cafeteria just after the bell rang for the lunch period. There was a rush of hungry students. Their feet made it sound like a stampede. Most of them were talking. Some were talking about their friends and things. Others were talking about schoolwork. Some were yelling and joking around. The smell of pizza was pouring out the cafeteria door, which made it hard to concentrate because Terry and I were both hungry. But we needed to do this assignment for Ms. Rogers, so we kept at it for the full five minutes. After most of the students went into the cafeteria, a few stragglers came along. They were scuffing their feet and laughing until Mr. Sennett told them to "Get a move on or you'll miss lunch." Terry and I recorded our observations on the sense chart until our five minutes were up, and then we went into the cafeteria so that we wouldn't miss lunch either.

For an appropriate follow-up exercise using this example, project it on a screen, rewrite it on a chalkboard or whiteboard, or distribute individual copies to students. Then ask the students to identify the answers to the who, what, when, where, why, and how questions. Did the writer complete the assignment faithfully? How might the paragraph be improved? If this paragraph represents the top layer of the inverted pyramid (called the lead in journalism), what information might be included in the next layer, the supporting details?

Students can extend the lesson individually and then discuss it, but it can be even more effective as a small-group or whole-class activity.

IDENTIFYING KEY IDEAS

The inverted pyramid can be a useful starting point to help visual, auditory, and kinesthetic learners identify key ideas and then to translate using other types of organization. For example, following is a typical newspaper lead, or first paragraph:

> Boats valued into the hundreds of thousands of dollars were about all that held up a collapsed dock roof Monday afternoon at the Tradewind Resort and Marina on Lake Ludlow. Sheets of twisted metal roof were compacted by snowdrifts along the roof's south side, and some boats could be seen sandwiched between water and roof. Many more were covered by the fallen roof—invisible to boaters looking on from the shore.

Using this example, the teacher might ask students, first, to answer who, what, when, where, why and how, which might be done by quoting from the paragraph as follows:

Who: boaters looking on from the shore

What: boats . . . sandwiched between water and roof

When: Monday afternoon

Where: Tradewind Resort and Marina on Lake Ludlow

Why: a collapsed dock roof

How: snowdrifts

The answers represent the key ideas. The purpose of using this journalistic form of organization is to put the key ideas up front. But there are six key questions. What is the central question, the most important of these? Students should be able to recognize it as the first few words of the opening sentence: "Boats valued into the hundreds of thousands of dollars." (Money is always a headline maker.)

The next step is to examine these ideas and consider how the news story might continue. Where do these key ideas lead? And how can teachers tie this exercise to previous developmental exercises, such as engaging the senses? One way is to ask students to use the sense exploration template (Figure 3.2) in conjunction with their who, what, when, where, why, and how responses to brainstorm plausible sensory details. Then, well equipped with descriptive words, the students can write the next paragraph or two of the news article. They will be creating fiction, of course, but they will do so in context by assuming the role of a news reporter. What might the reporter observe, and how might the reporter write the supporting-details paragraphs of this news article?

Visual learners will note that this lead paragraph contains mostly visual imagery. So for these learners, the task will be to identify the visuals, such as the collapsed dock roof, the twisted metal compacted by snow, and the "boats . . . sandwiched between water and roof." Could they add other visual elements?

For auditory and kinesthetic learners, the task will be to discern implicit sounds and movements in this visual description. These learners might brainstorm some of the following descriptions:

Auditory

> creaking metal roof
>
> angry voices of boat owners
>
> wind whipping and snapping canvas boat covers

Kinesthetic

> twisting metal
>
> rocking boats
>
> boaters balancing on the swaying dock

Using the main idea—boats worth a great deal of money are damaged by a collapsed dock roof—and the ideas based on the answers to the who, what, when, where, why, and how questions, students can create a reality-based fictional set of supporting details. The example that follows shows two paragraphs that might come after the factual lead:

> "My boat was worth $75,000," Joseph Crandall complained angrily. "And now it's a floating dock support, a broken hunk of junk." Crandall was one of several boat owners who balanced on the swaying dock, looking at the ruins of their boats and cursing their luck. The wind whipped the canvas boat coverings, many of which had been torn by the twisting metal as the roof collapsed. What remained of the roof lay creaking on the scattered, rocking boats. The boaters' cigarette smoke was acrid in the icy air and probably left a taste in their mouths as bitter as their disappointment that the

dock roof had been too weak to support the heavy snow that had fallen so quickly that morning.

By late Monday afternoon, most of the boaters had turned up their collars against the biting wind and left for their homes to call their insurance agents or maybe just to drown their sorrows and wait for spring.

In practice, teachers who use a newspaper lead formula can base a similar exercise on that text and then, after students have created their own paragraphs of supporting details, reveal what the next paragraphs in the newspaper story really were and ask students to compare their inventions to the reported facts. In so doing they will enhance the analytical element of this type of lesson.

ANOTHER TRANSLATION: FACTUAL REPORTAGE

In Chapter 3, I suggested that Bloom's taxonomy provides a way for teachers to move students toward higher-order thinking. This type of exercise—focused on identifying key ideas, using the inverted pyramid for organization, and drawing on students' experience with sense exploration—allows teachers to move students up the Bloom pyramid. Although the student writers are creating fiction, they are doing essentially what real reporters do in real situations: They look for the facts, the big ideas, and then they look for supporting information, details that make the facts clear and often give them a human face. This exercise requires not merely knowledge, comprehension, and application but also analysis and synthesis, as the students examine the facts and extrapolate to invent supporting details. The facts and the fictionalized details are synthesized to create an extension of the original news lead.

This exercise also can be used to recycle the observations called for in the sample lesson from Chapter 3 that then were used to introduce the inverted pyramid organization concept in a previous section of this chapter. Students might use their notes to draft descriptions and translate them into journalistic style by organizing a new draft in the inverted pyramid style. The previous descriptive paragraph might be transformed into something like the following:

> The aroma of pizza causes a stampede every lunch hour as hungry students race to the cafeteria after the bell rings. Most of them come talking about friends or schoolwork or yelling and joking around. Only a few straggle behind, scuffing their feet and laughing until Mr. Sennett says, "Get a move on or you'll miss lunch."

Terry Molnar and Alex Turner stood across the hallway from the main door to the cafeteria. Their job was to observe the daily stampede as part of a writing assignment for Ms. Rogers' English class. They took notes on what they saw, heard, smelled, felt, and tasted—or wanted to taste. The mouth-watering smell of pizza almost made them cut short the required five-minute observation time. They stayed on the job, but when the five minutes were up, they eagerly joined the stampede for fresh, hot pizza.

This paragraph, based on a factual, multisensory observation, might be included in a classroom or school newspaper. As I suggested in Chapter 2, writing authentically for real audiences is motivational. Teachers can make school writing more authentic, more like intentional adult writing, by considering assignments and contexts. In this instance an observation assignment used to help students learn how to use multisensory description can take on a secondary motivational aspect as a potential article for publication in a classroom or school newspaper or a parent newsletter. Keeping motivational aspects of assignments in mind is particularly valuable when working with students who are struggling to learn how to write well.

SAMPLE LESSON 4.1: GATHERING AND ORGANIZING INFORMATION

The following lesson draws on the ideas in this chapter and provides choices so that visual, auditory, and kinesthetic learners can work to their preferred learning style or explore another.

Background: Most writing requires two preliminary activities: (a) gathering some sort of information such as observing and reading followed by note-taking; and (b) organizing the information in order to present it in a manner that can be easily understood.

Assignment: Students may work singly, in pairs, or in triads to complete the first two steps. Then each student should individually create a draft text, which can be shared and may be further refined or simply left as a rough draft.

Step 1. Choose an information source from the following list and make notes, being certain to answer the who, what, when, where, why, and how questions:

    a. A short story or a scene within a short story.

    b. A scene from a television show or motion picture.

    c. A description from a history or science book of a particular action or event.

Step 2. Choose a way to organize the information from the following list and create a graphic organizer:

    a. Pearls-on-a-string organization.

    b. Inductive organization.

    c. Deductive organization.

    d. Inverted pyramid organization.

Step 3. Write a draft text—a descriptive report or a news article—based on the information as it has been organized.

Assessment: Students should share their drafts in pairs or small groups and respond to three questions:

1. Does the draft include information that answers the who, what, when, where, why, and how questions?

2. Is the manner of organization appropriate to the information?

3. Does the draft reflect the organizational plan?

The questions in this assignment can be difficult, especially the first time they are used. The teacher should consider some direct guidance for the whole class as a starting point, particularly in terms of matching the most appropriate form of organization to the available information (question 2) and then following the organizational plan when writing the draft (question 3). It is not unusual for students to create a graphic organizer and then write a draft that wholly ignores it. Writing from a plan, whether a list, an outline, or a graphic organizer, is a skill that must be taught; it does not come naturally for many students.

SAMPLE LESSON 4.2: ARTISTIC ORGANIZATION

This chapter has focused on organizing ideas in ways that matched the preferred learning styles of visual, auditory, and kinesthetic learners or allowed them to explore other learning styles to add to their repertoire of successful writing strategies.

Background: Most writing requires two preliminary activities: (a) some sort of information gathering, such as observing and reading followed by note-taking; and (b) organizing the information in order to present it in a manner that can be easily understood.

Assignment: Students may work singly, in pairs, or in triads to complete the first two steps. Then each student should individually create a text draft, which can be shared and may be further refined or simply left as a rough draft.

Step 1. Choose an information source from the following list and make notes, being certain to answer the who, what, when, where, why, and how questions:

   a. A description of a historical event, perhaps from a social studies textbook

   b. A scientific demonstration (A videotape, rather than a live demonstration, will allow for multiple observations.)

   c. A musical event such as a concert (Again, a videotape will allow for multiple observations.)

Step 2. Choose a way to organize the information from the following list and create a graphic organizer:

   a. Pearls-on-a-string organization

   b. Inductive organization

   c. Deductive organization

   d. Inverted pyramid organization

Step 3. Write a draft text—a descriptive report or a news article—based on the information as it has been organized.

Assessment: Students should share their drafts in pairs or small groups and respond to three questions:

1. Does the draft include information that answers the who, what, when, where, why, and how questions?

2. Is the manner of organization appropriate to the information?

3. Does the draft reflect the organizational plan?

5 Clarifying Ideas Using Walkabout Strategies

In discussing the sample lesson in Chapter 4, I mentioned that student writers sometimes experience a disconnect between planning and then drafting a piece of writing based on that plan. They can be like untrained cooks who merely glance at a recipe and then set the cookbook aside while they create their own dish, usually with disastrous results. Teachers of writing should keep in mind that most students need to be explicitly taught that the writing process is, in fact, a set of interconnected processes. The continuum of stimulus-process-product is represented in the arrow graphic (Figure 1.1). When the continuum is repeated or reiterated, it cycles back, as represented by the recycling graphic (Figure 1.2). Everything from initial stimulus to final product is focused on producing an effective written text.

The full import of this continuum is most easily grasped by linguistic and logical-mathematical learners, who can respond to its being taught as linear and logical. But the range of the continuum—and particularly all of the various internal connections that hold the processes together—may be less obvious to visual, auditory, and kinesthetic learners. These learners are more likely to grasp the interconnectedness of the writing process when nontraditional activities are used to match their learning styles.

However, teachers must teach how the process of organizing, drafting, and revising is part of a continuum, or these learners may see activities such as those described in the preceding chapters as discrete. Visual, auditory, and kinesthetic learners seem most likely to discard the directions without reading them and immediately set about making the model or putting together the bicycle, only to end up with a mess and calling for help. In particular, these students need activities that are tailored to their learning-style preferences and that help them master the intricacies of the writing process so that they can build fluency and a capacity for *informed spontaneity*. I refer to these as *see-say-and-do* activities because they involve the visual, auditory, and kinesthetic manipulation of text.

Informed spontaneity describes the skills of the experienced cook who makes cooking well look easy and food taste good because he or she has internalized information about ingredients, measurements, preparation, cooking temperatures, and so on. The experienced cook who can prepare a dish spontaneously, with merely a glance (if that) at the recipe, is informed by experience, study, and practice. The effective writer, the student who can respond to an assignment or a test prompt with easy competence also is employing informed spontaneity. The effective writer has internalized the writing process and can engage in mentally planning, even drafting, often automatically (to use Bloom's concept), so that the visible result is a complete and competent piece of writing.

Internalized understandings of a process come from practice and experimentation. In the preceding chapters I have introduced a number of concepts and lesson strategies, such as authenticity (writing about real things), multidimensional responses, sensory reportage and exploration, translations, various patterns of organization, writing up Bloom's taxonomy, and identifying main ideas and supporting details. This chapter will continue to build on these concepts and strategies by examining ways to help visual, auditory, and kinesthetic learners clarify ideas as they draft and revise their writing.

WALKABOUTS

In Australian aboriginal cultures, a *walkabout* describes a ritual in which a young man goes on a solitary journey through the wilderness to discover his character. Walkabouts are journeys of discovery, foremost of oneself but also of one's surroundings. The walkabout offers an apt metaphor for a similar process that should engage the thoughtful writer as he or she gathers information, arranges it in an organized manner, and turns that organization into text.

Teachers can use walkabouts in several ways, and three of these make a useful sequence. The first and most natural is the walkabout itself. The second is an abstract walkabout tailored for the visual, auditory, or kinesthetic learner. And the third is the walkabout within a paragraph, which I will take up separately as a revision strategy in the next section.

The physical walkabout incorporates all three of the see-say-and-do aspects. As in the observation exercise of the sample lesson in Chapter 3, students can be sent out singly or in pairs to walk about in a given area at a given time and to record their impressions. The teacher might say, "Choose an area where you can walk for about five minutes, say, from your house to the grocery store or some other familiar route. Jot down what you experience using the sense exploration template." This portion of the exercise will result in raw information for a written description, which students can plan using one of the organization techniques described in Chapter 4.

The key question, the question asked by the teacher that makes this a walkabout experience, is, "What did you discover about yourself, your feelings and perceptions, as a result of your walking observation?" This is the aspect of self-discovery, and it may be hard for students to engage in such introspection at first. It takes practice, and a bit of structure can be helpful. For example, the teacher might use the strategy illustrated in Chapter 3, when students were asked to describe their classroom prior to using the sense exploration template. In this case, they might be asked to think about the familiar walk before the structured observation and to write down their description as a *before* draft.

Using this sequence—pre-observation draft, walking observation, organization, new (or revised) draft—will help students spot the before-and-after differences, the new things they pick up on that were always there but previously went unnoticed. Here are two examples of reflections (excerpted from full descriptions):

> I never noticed the ramp at the side of the green house before. I don't think I've ever seen anyone use a wheelchair there. It made me wonder if someone in a wheelchair lives there or maybe lived there in the past. Maybe I'll look that way more often or just ask someone.

> The wind was out of the right direction when I walked down the street, so I could smell chocolate cooking from the candy factory a few blocks away. I hadn't thought much about it before, but I think I always smile when I smell that chocolate. It makes me feel good. I can almost taste it, especially on cold days.

Encouraging students to reflect on their walkabout observations in this way provides an engaging opportunity to introduce the concept of analysis. Remember that, according to Bloom's taxonomy, analysis implies separating concepts into component parts so that the structure or organization can be understood. Analysis asks and attempts to answer *why* questions. The student who notices the wheelchair ramp is asking, Why is it there? Does someone live there who uses a wheelchair? How can I find out? The student who notices the smell of chocolate coming from the nearby candy factory is asking, Why do I notice the aroma? How does it make me feel?

It is not a huge leap to use this strategy in a second, less personal, more abstract way. But it helps if students have had some experience with personal walkabouts. The second type of walkabout can be tailored specifically for visual, auditory, and kinesthetic learning. For example, a student engaged in a visual walkabout might look at a realistic painting of a room or a street, or a photograph of an indoor or outdoor scene. The student attempts to imagine that he or she can, like the characters in a motion picture (*Mary Poppins* is an example), simply drop into the scene and walk about, making the same kinds of observations that might be made in a real situation. Remember that key analysis words include *appraise, calculate, categorize, compare, contrast, criticize,* and *distinguish.* They imply the kinds of thinking that students can be led to do. The teacher might ask, "What elements are familiar and unfamiliar in the scene? If you walked into this place, how might you feel? What would make you feel this way?"

Consider what might occur if students viewed a reproduction of American painter Thomas Eakins's 1889 portrayal of an anatomy lesson in *The Agnew Clinic* (available online at www.artchive.com/artchive/E/eakins/eakins_agnew.jpg.html), or a photograph of Thomas Edison in his workshop (available online at www.hfmgv.org/research/photo/jit/still/catalog/B/B.99552_large.jpg). Students might consider the progress in scientific contexts: How is the practice of medicine different today as compared to the late 1800s? What tools are evident in Edison's workshop, and how might he have employed them as an inventor? If I were in the audience at the anatomy lesson or standing with Edison in his workshop, how might I feel? Applications across the curriculum can be developed using visual images related to science, history, literature, the arts, technology, and so on.

Auditory learners can make their walkabouts while listening to an audio documentary or an audio book. Recordings of old-time radio comedies and dramas are excellent walkabout destinations and readily obtainable in libraries and bookstores. So are recordings of famous speeches. Students should ask themselves, What sense images are conjured up by the narration, dialogue, and sound effects I hear? If the recording is, for instance, a National Public Radio (NPR) travelogue about an Amazon adventure, the student will hear the calls of wild birds and the sound of water lapping against the sides of the boat. The student might ask, How would I feel on such an adventure? What could I discover about myself? How might I be challenged or changed?

Kinesthetic learners can walk about by participating in skits or scenes from stage plays. One student can take on all of the roles, or two or three students can work together. The idea is that they not merely sit and read the script but get up and act it out with script in hand: a process called a walk-through. Students might ask, What would my character be thinking and feeling? How should I move to show those thoughts and feelings? What tone of voice should I use? The sense exploration template is valuable in this context as well, so that students can document the sense impressions that would come through the scene if it had occurred in their lives. Are the characters conversing over a meal in a diner, for instance? Given this situation, what are the sounds, sights, smells, and tastes? If the students mime eating and drinking, what tactile characteristics must they convey?

The more fully these abstract walkabouts can be imagined, the richer the experience will be—and the more fully developed the *after* texts will be.

PARAGRAPH WALKABOUTS

The third walkabout strategy is specifically tailored to revising an existing text. All writing is revision, according to the maxim about writing. All revision is analysis and synthesis. Students will be asked to walk about in a paragraph, observing the surroundings—the sentences—and making decisions about the impressions created by sentence order, pattern, detail, and rhythm. One of the examples from Chapter 4 will serve as the basis:

> Terry and I decided to stand in the hallway across from the main door to the cafeteria just after the bell rang for the lunch period. There was a rush of hungry students. Their feet made it sound like a stampede. Most of them were talking. Some were talking about their friends and things. Others were talking about schoolwork. Some were yelling and joking around. The smell of pizza was pouring out the cafeteria door, which made it hard to concentrate because Terry and I were both hungry. But we needed to do this assignment for Ms. Rogers, so we kept at it for the full five minutes. After most of the students went into the cafeteria, a few stragglers came along. They were scuffing their feet and laughing until Mr. Sennett told them to "Get a move on or you'll miss lunch." Terry and I recorded our observations on the sense chart until our five minutes were up, and then we went into the cafeteria so that we wouldn't miss lunch either.

The paragraph walkabout exercise will be most effective if the teacher first presents it as a whole-class discussion, using an overhead projector or some other visual means to make the entire lesson visible. Simple chart paper will do, in fact. The first step in a paragraph walkabout is to take the paragraph apart by listing the sentences in order:

1. Terry and I decided to stand in the hallway across from the main door to the cafeteria just after the bell rang for the lunch period.

2. There was a rush of hungry students.

3. Their feet made it sound like a stampede.

4. Most of them were talking.

5. Some were talking about their friends and things.

6. Others were talking about schoolwork.

7. Some were yelling and joking around.

8. The smell of pizza was pouring out the cafeteria door, which made it hard to concentrate because Terry and I were both hungry.

9. But we needed to do this assignment for Ms. Rogers, so we kept at it for the full five minutes.

10. After most of the students went into the cafeteria, a few stragglers came along.

11. They were scuffing their feet and laughing until Mr. Sennett told them to "Get a move on or you'll miss lunch."

12. Terry and I recorded our observations on the sense chart until our five minutes were up, and then we went into the cafeteria so that we wouldn't miss lunch either.

After the paragraph is separated into the list of sentences, the teacher should ask, "What do you observe about the sentences?" Students will offer a variety of responses. For example:

"Some sentences are long, some are short."

"Sentences 2 through 7 are all short. There's no variety. It seems choppy."

"Only sentence 8 says how the writer is feeling."

"We don't know until sentence 9 why the writer and Terry are doing this."

Students' responses should be written down because they will form the basis for the next stage of the revision. The teacher should lead a discussion of the observations. For instance, is the remark "Some sentences are long, some are short" positive, neutral, or negative? The teacher can help students understand that sentence variety is a positive but that balancing longer and shorter sentences is part of the equation. So when six sentences in a row are short, "It seems choppy" is a valid negative criticism. (This can be a teachable moment to introduce or review simple, compound, and complex sentence structures.)

Once students have analyzed their observations, the next step will be to work as a group to change the sentences to address the negative criticism. It is important for this process to be transparent so that students can see exactly how the revised draft is created. The following edited paragraph illustrates how the revision might be accomplished. (Words, phrases, and sentences that have been moved or added are italicized, and strike-throughs show those deleted.)

> Terry and I *needed to do a five-minute observation assignment for Ms. Rogers. We* decided to stand in the hallway across from the main door to the cafeteria just after the bell rang for the lunch period. The smell of pizza ~~was~~ pouring out the cafeteria door~~, which~~ made it hard to concentrate. There was a rush of hungry students~~. Their~~ *whose* feet ~~made it~~ sound*ed* like a stampede. Most of ~~them~~ *the students* were talk-ing~~. Some were talking~~ about their friends and things. *Some were yelling and joking around.* Others were talking about schoolwork. ~~Some were yelling and joking around. The smell of pizza was pouring out the cafeteria door, which made it hard to concentrate because Terry and I were both hungry. But we needed to do this assignment for Ms. Rogers, so we kept at it for the full five minutes.~~ After most of the students went into the cafeteria, a few stragglers came along. They were scuffing their feet and laughing until Mr. Sennett told them, ~~to~~ "Get a move on or you'll miss lunch." Terry and I recorded our observations on the sense chart until our five minutes were up, and then we went into the cafeteria so that we wouldn't miss lunch ~~either~~.

In the revised paragraph, the students have slightly changed the order of the sentences, combined some of the short sentences into longer ones, and changed some of the wording. Their revisions give the paragraph a more logical flow, and the sentences no longer seem choppy.

AUDITORY AND KINESTHETIC PARAGRAPH WALKABOUTS

The paragraph walkabout described in the preceding section is largely a linguistic-visual exercise. Auditory and kinesthetic learners will benefit from a couple of adaptations to the initial experience. That way, all learn-ers can add to their repertoire of revision strategies.

The first adaptation involves reading aloud. When students read aloud their own and other students' writing, all students, regardless of preferred learning style, are helped. Sometimes writers can hear problems that they don't see. Following are three suggestions that extend the previous lesson:

1. Read the paragraph aloud. Listen and respond: Do the ideas flow logically? Are the sentences interesting and informative or incomplete and choppy?

2. Read each sentence in the list. Listen and respond: Does the sentence sound "right"? Are the sentences in the best possible order?

3. Read the revised paragraph aloud. Listen and respond: Is it an improvement over the first draft? Do changes still need to be made?

As students gain experience with the paragraph walkabout and these read-aloud adaptations, the teacher can move from whole-class to small-group practice. Pairs of students can analyze and revise together, one serving as the reader and the other as the listener-responder. The teacher should encourage the students to trade roles periodically.

Kinesthetic learners will benefit from a different adaptation, one that involves movement and action. This adaptation consists of writing down the component sentences and using a scissors to cut the individual sentences apart. During whole-class instruction, the teacher and a couple of volunteer students can do this using large sheets of chart or butcher paper. The strips of sentences can then be re-ordered, divided, and taped together, physically accomplishing the same goal as the visual revision process. This process also can help free linguistic, visual, and auditory learners to manipulate text more aggressively than they might otherwise do.

Many students are timid revisers, at least at first, until they internalize the notion that all writing truly is revision. Humorist James Thurber usually is given credit for the aphorism, "The only good writing is rewriting." Sometimes it helps if the teacher will parse the word *revision* for students. The teacher can explain that *revise* literally means to "re-see," that is, to see the piece of writing with new eyes or in a new light. Revising is not, as students and naive writers often assume, a matter of correcting minor errors. The kinesthetic strategy is an effective way to push students to revise more thoroughly. Students need to understand that it is all right— indeed, often necessary—to "rip into" a piece of writing in order to revise it and make it the best it can be.

COLLABORATIVE PLANNING, DRAFTING, AND REVISING

In many of the activities described in this book, I suggest allowing students to work in pairs or small groups. Collaborative writing restructures the writing process, transforming it from an often solitary activity into a cooperative experience. Students learn from one another, and pairing them across learning styles (rather than matching students with the same learning style) can be helpful in increasing their repertoires of planning, drafting, and revising strategies.

The practice of authentic writing, which I discussed in Chapter 2, finds resonance in collaborative writing. The practice should not be confined to the language arts classroom. In fact, it is an ideal strategy in science and social studies classes, where students often are asked to undertake fairly major research assignments. Tackling a complex scientific investigation using teams is a common practice in real-world laboratories. Collaborative writing can be used to support such an investigation by giving students a chance to work as teams, just as they might be called on to do in a professional laboratory setting. Moreover, this strategy works as well with third-graders and their bean seedlings as it does with high school juniors attempting to measure the amount of oxygen in air.

With collaborative writing, students learn from each other, sometimes in novel ways. The process encourages students to verbalize about writing itself as well as about the subject of the writing assignment—certainly a plus for auditory learners. Students are able to share ideas and problems and work toward a mutually satisfying product. The process helps students elaborate on initial ideas (which can boost the content and complexity of planning), voice and support their opinions, and evaluate new information and ideas—all skills with which beginning writers tend to have difficulties. Collaborative writing tends to move students up the pyramid of Bloom's taxonomy.

Getting students to work together effectively and efficiently is the first instructional challenge. The following five guidelines may be useful:

1. *Establish groups.* Collaborative writing—whether planning, drafting, revising, or a combination of these—is most effectively accomplished by a pair of students or no more than a group of three. In larger groups the logistics of organizing the writing process tend to become unwieldy, especially with younger students. Some teachers permit students to find their own partners; others prefer to pair students whose interests or personalities seem compatible. Either procedure can work, depending on the nature of the lesson.

2. *Set ground rules.* The watchword in collaborative writing is *cooperation.* The students must learn to focus on the writing task, not the personalities of their partners. The contributions of each member of the group are important, and criticism must be directed at ideas, not people. Effective group work in the classroom depends on the teacher's setting a we-are-all-in-this-together tone. Ground rules along these lines should

be brief, explicitly stated (preferably in writing), clearly understood, and enforced.

3. *Match assignment to experience.* Collaborative writing tasks should match both the writing levels of the students and their experience with group work. It is tempting to reason that two (or three) heads are better than one and to assign more complex tasks for group work. This is a mistake (and could be disastrous) because the process of working as a pair or small group is itself a heady challenge. Initially, group assignments should be only as difficult as an assignment that a student might be expected to do individually. Later, with more experience, students will be able to undertake more challenging work.

4. *Set time limits.* Collaborative projects tend to take more time than individual assignments. Plan for the three Gs: *gathering, groping, grouping.* It takes time for groups to gather, to get acquainted and to figure out how the group experience is supposed to work. Next, the group will spend time groping, trying to understand the assignment and their roles in getting the work done. Finally, there is grouping, that period when the group actually is focused and functioning effectively together. Setting realistic time limits will help groups work through these stages and stay on target.

5. *Formulate accountability.* Central to the cooperative spirit of collaborative writing is that the group is accountable: the idea that we are all in this together. While grouping can be effective as a means of helping individuals work toward their own individual products, the intent in the form of collaboration I am describing is to produce a single group product—a coauthored or coedited text, if you will. Therefore, evaluation must focus on the group's process. What elements were successful? Which needed more work? No one is alone in a collaborative experience. The key idea embodied in collaboration is that group support will help prevent individual failure.

GUIDE ON THE SIDE

Someone during the early days of promoting facilitative teaching coined the notion that in many instances a teacher can be more effective as a guide on the side, rather than a sage on the stage. When teachers work with students to help them clarify ideas through hands-on, see-say-and-do activities, whether individually or collaboratively, they will likely be more helpful as guides on the side.

The walkabouts and collaborative processes involve students in making discoveries about themselves and others. In particular, group work adds to the kinds of decisions that students must make, for one of a group's first decisions will be to decide who does what. Some groups simply divide the tasks, with each student being responsible for a portion. In other groups, students work on the whole project together with each individual participating as needed. One group may designate a recorder; in another, everyone might take a hand in writing.

As students work together, questions must be asked by the individual: How am I doing? Am I doing the best that I can? Am I contributing to the work of the group? Remember, part of the walkabout concept is that walking about, physically or more abstractly tailored to sensory input, is intended to be a journey of self-discovery. Students need to discover how they learn most effectively and how those effective learning strategies can be applied to writing and ultimately transferred to learning in other contexts. (This process is called *metacognition*, learning about learning.)

At the same time, collaboration also will be strengthened if students are encouraged to engage in group self-assessment. While some ways of working are more effective than others, it is important that group members evaluate their group's methods of operation and come to their own conclusions. Teachers can assist by suggesting ways of working but should refrain from rigid prescriptions. Eventually, pairs or triads that are allowed to work together over time will develop singular working relationships that capitalize on the strengths of individual members.

In collaborative writing and walkabout activities, once the initial groundwork has been laid through direct instruction, effective supervision is done from a distance. Observing individual students and general supervision can be accomplished discreetly to allow everyone to exercise a responsible degree of freedom. Occasional prodding may be necessary to keep an individual student or a group on task, but often it can be done through asking questions rather than issuing orders. The teacher might ask: "What are you working on now? How did you arrive at that decision? Have you considered other ways of accomplishing X?" Such questions challenge students to think through their writing projects. In responding, the students will steer back on course; and their answers, in many cases, will help the teacher keep track of their progress. The teacher's role is not to direct the work but to ensure that individuals and groups are productive on their own.

SAMPLE LESSON 5.1: PARAGRAPH WALKABOUT AND SENSE EXPLORATION

The following lesson focuses on the paragraph walkabout described in this chapter and integrates a sense exploration activity that should help visual, auditory, and kinesthetic learners approach the activity effectively.

Background: The samples below are paragraphs from two responses to this assignment: Describe an activity that you enjoy seeing or doing.

Horsemanship competition is simply doing things with the horse to show how well you have control over the horse. What I did was first ride the horse at a walking pace (around 2 mph), the second task that I completed was to ride the horse at a jog (around 4 mph), the third thing that I had to do was to ride the horse at a trot (around 6 mph), and the last test that I had to complete was to keep the horse under control at a lope (approximately 8 mph).

Hiking is a great activity to get into. You always get to go outdoors and have fresh air while hiking, which is healthy for you. It also supplies a great source of exercise to keep you fit. Besides that, there are a lot of other good things about hiking too, like the silence of a deep woods or a noisy, insect-filled prairie. You can see amazing things when you are hiking, like a plant growing, flowers blooming brilliant colors, glistening snow, and shimmering water. While hiking, you can also watch for many animals in all four seasons. Hiking is an enjoyable, and my favorite, activity.

Assignment: Students should work in pairs or triads to choose either of these paragraphs and complete the following steps in a paragraph walkabout revision:

1. Rewrite the sentences in the paragraph as a list.

2. Analyze the sentences by answering the following questions:
   a. What do you observe about the individual sentences? Characterize your observations as positive, neutral, or negative.
   b. Does the writer use various types of sentences (simple, compound, complex)?
   c. Are the sentences in a logical order? If not, how might they be rearranged? (Physically or in your imagination, walk through the description to check for logical order.) Check for appropriate use of transition words.

3. Consider the sensory reportage aspects of the paragraph by using a sense exploration template (Figure 3.2) to record the sensory information used by the writer. Are some senses missing? Are some overused?

4. Revise the paragraph by doing the following:

   a. Change the sentences that you viewed as negative.

   b. Adjust the sentence variety if necessary.

   c. Reorder the sentences or ideas so that the information flows logically.

   d. Balance the sensory information, adding or deleting aspects of sensory reportage as necessary.

5. Read the revised paragraph to yourself and to a classmate. Does it sound better?

Assessment: Students should share their revisions with their classmates and look for similarities and differences. For an extension of this lesson, the teacher can post or project (using an overhead or LCD) two or three of the revised paragraphs side by side and then lead a whole-class discussion of the merits of the various revisions.

This paragraph-walkabout lesson is ideal for focusing on paragraphs written by students. When this procedure is followed, it can be helpful (and avoid potential embarrassment) to use unidentified samples from other classes—at least at first. Later, after students have become comfortable with sharing and revising their work with their peers, samples from their own classmates' papers will make this exercise even more meaningful.

Like most lessons, this one bears repeating in order to help students understand and be able to use the revision strategies well. But the steps also can be isolated for focused reinforcement of various aspects of the process.

SAMPLE LESSON 5.2: PARAGRAPH WALKABOUT ANALYSIS

This lesson uses a sense exploration activity to help visual, auditory, and kinesthetic learners hone their analysis skills.

Background: The paragraph below is based on the prompt: Briefly describe the life and major work of a famous person in history.

Louis Pasteur was born into a family of a tannery. When he was born his father was a noncommissioned officer in the army of Napoleon and had received the Legion of Honor from the emperor himself. As a child, he showed no great interest in science. In fact, he showed potential as an artist, and it was in that field where most of his interest was. He ended up studying chemistry in Paris, where he found out what was really for him. In 1849, at the age of 27, Louis Pasteur began studying fermentation, a type of chemical breakdown of substances by microbes, as a professor in Strasbourg, France. Pasteur will never be forgotten for it was he who first discovered that most diseases are spread and caused by bacteria, or germs.

Assignment: Students should work in pairs or triads to choose one of these paragraphs and complete the following steps in a paragraph walkabout revision:

1. Rewrite the sentences in the paragraph as a list.

2. Analyze the sentences by answering the following questions:
   a. What do you observe about the individual sentences? Characterize your observations as positive, neutral, or negative.
   b. Does the writer use various types of sentences (simple, compound, complex)?
   c. Are the sentences in a logical order? If not, how might they be rearranged? (Physically or in your imagination, walk through the description to check for logical order.) Check for appropriate use of transition words.

3. Consider the sensory reportage aspects of the paragraph by using a sense exploration template (Figure 3.2) to record the sensory information used by the writer. Are some senses missing? Are some overused?

4. Revise the paragraph by doing the following:
   a. Change the sentences that you viewed as negative.
   b. Adjust the sentence variety if necessary.
   c. Reorder the sentences or ideas so that the information flows logically.
   d. Balance the sensory information, adding or deleting aspects of sensory reportage as necessary.

5. Read the revised paragraph to yourself and to a classmate. Does it sound better?

Assessment: Students should share their revisions with their classmates and look for similarities and differences. For an extension of this lesson, the teacher can post or project two or three of the revised paragraphs side by side and then lead a whole-class discussion of the merits of the various revisions.

6 Using Patterns and Rhythms for Writing Sense

The paragraph walkabout introduced in Chapter 5 can attune visual, auditory, and kinesthetic learners to conventional patterns and rhythms that make writing more pleasing to read and give the reader better access to the writer's meaning and intent. To expand the focus on patterns and rhythms, consider:

> Four score and seven years ago, our fathers brought forth upon this continent a new nation, conceived in liberty, and dedicated to the proposition that all men are created equal.

How much more powerful, almost poetic is Lincoln's opening of the *Gettysburg Address*, than if he had written: "Eighty-seven years ago our country was founded on the principle of liberty and the idea that everyone is equal." Such a translation is certainly direct and modern, but it wrings out the emotion that Lincoln deliberately set into the speech and then so eloquently reinforced in the closing sentence, where he rhythmically repeats its phrasing:

> . . . that this nation, under God, shall have a new birth of freedom; and that government *of the people, by the people*, and *for the people*, shall not perish from the earth. [italics added]

When we see these words on paper, we see a pattern. And when we hear them, we hear the rhythm of the writer's language. Patterns and rhythms are important to consider when working with students on developing high-level writing skills.

Visual and auditory learners will relate well to considering writing in terms of patterns and rhythms. And speeches, particularly those that students have seen delivered, whether by a famed speaker or an actor, resonate for kinesthetic learners, who will notice how gestures, facial expressions, and movements give power to the language. Two examples of speeches, readily available as video clips, come immediately to mind.

One is President John F. Kennedy's inaugural address in 1961, when he said, "And so, my fellow Americans: *Ask not what* your country can do for you—*ask what* you can do for your country." He emphasized his point about self-sacrifice and love of country by using rhythmic pairings (my italics).

Another is Martin Luther King, Jr.'s speech he delivered at the March on Washington on August 28, 1963, which repeats the phrase *I have a dream*.

> *I have a dream that one day* this nation will rise up and live out the true meaning of its creed. . . . *I have a dream that one day* . . . the sons of former slaves and the sons of former slaveowners will be able to sit down together at a table of brotherhood. *I have a dream that one day* even the state of Mississippi . . . will be transformed into an oasis of freedom and justice. *I have a dream* that my four children will one day live in a nation where they will not be judged by the color of their skin but by the content of their character. *I have a dream today.* [italics added]

We remember these famous speeches not only because of the momentous events and larger-than-life individuals to which they are connected, not only because they are eloquent expressions of noble ideas but also because the patterns and rhythms of these texts give the words power and make the ideas they convey transparent.

DISCERNING AND ADJUSTING PATTERNS AND RHYTHMS

An example from the sample lesson in Chapter 5 makes a good starting point to show how teachers can work with students and help them discern and adjust patterns and rhythms in their written drafts. The unrevised paragraph in the sample lesson read as follows:

> Horsemanship competition is simply doing things with the horse to show how well you have control over the horse. What I did was

first ride the horse at a walking pace (around 2 mph), the second task that I completed was to ride the horse at a jog (around 4 mph), the third thing that I had to do was to ride the horse at a trot (around 6 mph), and the last test that I had to complete was to keep the horse under control at a lope (approximately 8 mph).

The first problem that students notice, though often not before they have written the paragraph as a list of sentences (part of the paragraph walkabout strategy), is that there really are only two sentences in this paragraph, according to the punctuation:

1. Horsemanship competition is simply doing things with the horse to show how well you have control over the horse.

2. What I did was first ride the horse at a walking pace (around 2 mph), the second task that I completed was to ride the horse at a jog (around 4 mph), the third thing that I had to do was to ride the horse at a trot (around 6 mph), and the last test that I had to complete was to keep the horse under control at a lope (approximately 8 mph).

Most students will readily grasp that the second sentence is, in fact, a long run-on sentence that can be easily repunctuated as four separate, shorter sentences:

1. Horsemanship competition is simply doing things with the horse to show how well you have control over the horse.

2. What I did was first ride the horse at a walking pace (around 2 mph).

3. The second task that I completed was to ride the horse at a jog (around 4 mph).

4. The third thing that I had to do was to ride the horse at a trot (around 6 mph).

5. And the last test that I had to complete was to keep the horse under control at a lope (approximately 8 mph).

This listing strategy is primarily visual and thus ideal for visual learners; they can see patterns more readily in this manner. Asking students to read the sentences aloud will incorporate an auditory component; auditory learners will be more attuned to hearing rhythms, the sound counterparts to visual patterns. Asking students to write the sentences on strips of chart paper so that the words can be physically manipulated will add a kinesthetic component. Kinesthetic learners will respond to this hands-on strategy and thus will more readily manipulate text in this manner than they will if they only see and hear the words.

In the three famous examples at the start of this chapter, the writers used rhythmic parallels to strengthen meaning. Visual and auditory (seen when read and heard) parallelism connects ideas. Even though the student writing about horsemanship has used correct transitional language—first, second, third, and last—this writer has not used the transition words in parallel phrases. In discussing this example, having previously discussed the parallel phrasing in examples such as the famous quotations, the teacher might ask, "How can sentences 2, 3, 4, and 5 be rephrased to use the transition words in similar, or parallel, phrases?"

Students should, with assistance at first, be able to revise the sentences along the following lines:

> Sentence 2. ~~What I did was first ride~~ *First, I rode* the horse at a walking pace (around 2 mph).

> Sentence 3. ~~The second task that I completed was to ride~~ *Second, I rode* the horse at a jog (around 4 mph).

> Sentence 4. ~~The third thing that I had to do was to ride~~ *Third, I rode* the horse at a trot (around 6 mph).

> Sentence 5. ~~And the last test that I had to complete was to keep the horse under control~~ *Last,* I rode at a lope (approximately 8 mph).

Next, the teacher might ask a student to read the revised paragraph aloud and then ask, "Does this sound better?" "Yes *and* no" is the response to look for. Yes, the parallel structure is in place, and so the pattern works. It is logical. But. . . . "Listen carefully to the rhythm," the teacher might advise. The rhythm of Martin Luther King's "I Have a Dream" speech is pounding because he is driving home an idea. In the revised paragraph, that short, pounding rhythm simply thuds along without adding meaning: "First, I rode"; "Second, I rode"; "Third, I rode"; "Last, I rode." How can the writer preserve the parallel structure but soften this dull, thudding rhythm?

This is an excellent topic for analysis because an overarching instructional goal is to help student writers resist the urge to grasp at formulaic responses. Just as there is no single, correct writing process, there also is no single formula for creating appropriate rhythms and patterns. Appropriateness depends on the writer's intent and the subject matter.

The teacher can lead students to brainstorm several revision ideas, and then ask pairs or small groups of students to try out their ideas and read the resulting revised paragraphs to the whole class. Writing the revised paragraphs on chart paper and posting them around the classroom so that all students can see one another's revisions works well at every grade level.

A couple of solutions to the problem come readily to mind. One way to reduce the thud factor is to add detail. Even in King's "I Have a Dream"speech, a good deal happens textually between the iterations. Here is an example using added detail to adjust the rhythm without changing the basic pattern:

> First, I rode at a walking pace. Holding my horse to a walk at about 2 miles per hour was not easy. And it also was hard to let the horse gradually speed up. Second, I rode at a jog, which was just a little faster, about 4 miles per hour. My horse wanted to go faster, but I kept control. Third, I rode at a trot. A trotting horse is going about 6 miles per hour, which is a pretty comfortable speed. Last, I rode at a lope, an easy 8 miles per hour, which is a fast, open speed for my horse but still much slower than a full-out gallop.

Adding detail gives the paragraph some breathing space between the parallel elements. The details also amplify the meaning.

Another way to adjust the rhythm is to use transition words that are not as specific. After all, the points in this paragraph, even in its revised form, are not highly developed—not to the extent that numbering the points is essential. The sequence of events can be easily understood without using sequential numbers. The following is the revision as softened by using different transition terms:

> *At first*, I rode at a walking pace. Holding my horse to a walk at about 2 miles per hour was not easy. And it also was hard to let the horse gradually speed up. *Next*, I rode at a jog, which was just a little faster, about 4 miles per hour. My horse wanted to go faster, but I kept control. *Then*, I rode at a trot. A trotting horse is going about 6 miles per hour, which is a pretty comfortable speed. *Finally*, I rode at a lope, an easy 8 miles per hour, which is a fast, open speed for my horse but still much slower than a full-out gallop.

At first, next, then, and *finally* are visually and auditorily less insistent than a numbered sequence. This change, along with the addition of more detail, makes for a paragraph that has a balanced, parallel, sequential structure but does not sound as though the writer is beating a drum to emphasize each point. The softer transition terms still help the reader to understand the events and their order, and the details flesh out the writer's descriptions of those events.

(Note: In the revised paragraphs, miles per hour has been written out rather than abbreviated. This small correction is important because it accurately tells the reader how to read the text. When reading the original paragraph aloud, should the reader say 2 mph or 2 miles per hour? Skillful writers do not leave interpretation to chance.)

TRANSLATING THE VISUAL AND THE AUDITORY FOR KINESTHETIC LEARNING

While visual and auditory learners are examining the pattern of the words they see and hear, kinesthetic learners will be equally attuned to how these patterns and rhythms translate into mental images of movement and action. The teacher might amplify this aspect of the discussion for visual and auditory learners (and linguistic-logical learners as well) by asking, "What details convey images of the writer/rider's actions? Are there other elements of sensory reportage that would strengthen these images? Choose sentence examples and discuss how they might be given more life." An example: "My horse wanted to go faster, but I kept control."

How did the horse show it wanted to go faster? What did the rider do to keep control? Students might add details in responding to these questions: My horse wanted to go faster. *I felt her push her head forward, trying to stretch out her neck for a run.* But I kept control *by holding tightly to the reins and squeezing with my legs.*

Notice the description of the movements: "push her head forward," "stretch out her neck," "holding tightly to the reins," and "squeezing with my legs." These are actions that form mental images.

There is a dictum in descriptive writing: Don't just tell. Show. These added images show the reader the actions behind the writer's statements. Even when the description is not directly related to a physical activity such as horseback riding, action and movement can be introduced to provide kinesthetic imagery that enlivens the writing and extends the writer's meaning by helping the reader create mental pictures. In King's "I Have a Dream" speech, for example, he provides concrete images on which to fasten his philosophy:

> I have a dream that one day this nation will *rise up and live out* the true meaning of its creed. . . . I have a dream that one day . . . the sons of former slaves and the sons of former slaveowners will be able to *sit down together* at a table of brotherhood. I have a dream that one day even the state of Mississippi . . . will *be transformed* into an oasis of freedom and justice. [italics added]

"Rise up and live out," "sit down together," and "be transformed" are active descriptions that create images of movement, which reinforce King's central message of necessary brotherhood. Kinesthetic imagery bolsters the power of patterns and rhythms to make a writer's meaning transparent.

BREVITY, ELABORATION, AND CONCEPTUAL DENSITY

An aspect of writing that is related to seeing and hearing patterns and rhythms is conceptual density—that is, how closely together important ideas are set in a piece of writing. In the unedited paragraph about horsemanship, although the information is relatively simple, the important ideas are tightly packed:

> Horsemanship competition is simply doing things with the horse to show how well you have control over the horse. What I did was first ride the horse at a walking pace (around 2 mph), the second task that I completed was to ride the horse at a jog (around 4 mph), the third thing that I had to do was to ride the horse at a trot (around 6 mph), and the last test that I had to complete was to keep the horse under control at a lope (approximately 8 mph).

We can ignore the fact that the second sentence is a long run-on and concentrate on the four concepts related to terms and speeds that are packed into only 73 words. Within this space the reader needs to understand *walking pace, jog, trot,* and *lope* and the speeds in miles per hour associated with each of these terms. That is dense conceptually, but the concepts are not complex.

Finding a balance point between brevity and elaboration often comes down to deciding how conceptually dense a piece of writing should be. If the ideas are complex, the writing should provide greater elaboration: in other words, less conceptual density, to ensure the reader's understanding.

In the example piece on horsemanship, the revision introduced greater elaboration, adjusting the pattern and rhythm of the paragraph by adding detail and kinesthetic imagery. Such elaboration increased the length of the full paragraph from 92 to 132 words:

> Horsemanship competition is simply doing things with the horse to show how well you have control over the horse. At first, I rode at a walking pace. Holding my horse to a walk at about 2 miles per

hour was not easy. And it also was hard to let the horse gradually speed up. Next, I rode at a jog, which was just a little faster, about 4 miles per hour. My horse wanted to go faster, but I kept control. Then, I rode at a trot. A trotting horse is going about 6 miles per hour, which is a pretty comfortable speed. Finally, I rode at a lope, an easy 8 miles per hour, which is a fast, open speed for my horse but still much slower than a full-out gallop.

The breathing space provided by the increased elaboration also reduced the conceptual density of the paragraph. Elaboration not only adds descriptive elements that increase a reader's understanding, but it also gives the reader more time to understand the concepts.

The principle of elaboration also can be applied to expanding a draft, for example, from a single paragraph to a longer composition. If the revised horsemanship paragraph above is again separated into individual sentences and those sentences are grouped, then students can readily see the opportunities for further development:

Horsemanship competition is simply doing things with the horse to show how well you have control over the horse. *What is horsemanship? What are the "things" in brief that will let the reader anticipate more information?*

At first, I rode at a walking pace. Holding my horse to a walk at about two miles per hour was not easy. And it also was hard to let the horse gradually speed up. *Why wasn't holding the horse to a walk easy? What made it difficult? Why is letting the horse speed up gradually hard?*

Next, I rode at a jog, which was just a little faster, about four miles per hour. My horse wanted to go faster, but I kept control. *Do horses always want to go fast? How did the writer keep control?*

Then, I rode at a trot. A trotting horse is going about six miles per hour, which is a pretty comfortable speed. *Why is trotting a comfortable speed? Comfortable for the rider or for the horse?*

Finally, I rode at a lope, an easy eight miles per hour, which is a fast, open speed for my horse but still much slower than a full-out gallop. *Is loping a fast, open speed for just the writer's horse or for horses in general? Would galloping be required to demonstrate horsemanship? How fast is a gallop?*

By responding to the questions in terms of detail, such as sensory reportage and kinesthetic imagery, students can develop each sentence cluster into a separate paragraph. This elaboration will yield a longer composition about horsemanship. This process also shows a way to get started on a longer composition by first summarizing the information in a single, well-constructed paragraph, which then can be developed by elaboration through the manipulation of detail.

OUTLINING TO REVISE

In Chapter 5, I specifically omitted outlining as a planning strategy because it is largely a linear-linguistic process. Visual, auditory, and kinesthetic learners usually are not comfortable using a formal outline for planning for this reason. Often it is easier for these learners to conceptualize in ways that better match their learning styles.

However, as visual, auditory, and kinesthetic learners revise, they work more and more toward linear and linguistic solutions to compositional challenges. Outlining can be used most effectively during revision. It is equally appropriate to use, possibly for a second time, with linguistic-logical learners who may have used an outline to plan their draft initially.

Formal outlines follow simple rules that are easy to master. The value of a formal outline lies in following these rules to achieve order, consistency, and balance. Figure 6.1 shows the standard order for levels of information detail. There is seldom any need for more than four levels in student work, although sophisticated, scholarly composition sometimes employs more levels, which are not shown in this figure.

Beyond this ordering of levels of detail, the other main rule of outlining relates to consistency and balance: No element of organization stands alone: Never a I without a II, never an A without a B, and so on. The descriptions can be words or phrases (a topic outline), as shown in Figure 6.1, or complete sentences (a sentence outline). Because outlining to revise is based on examining an existing text, creating a sentence outline may be easier for students to do and will look more complete than a topic outline will look.

Balance usually can be discerned at a glance by simply looking at the levels of detail. For example, the teacher might direct students to look at the wordless outline below and ask, "Is the composition reflected in this outline likely to be conceptually balanced?"

Figure 6.1	Outline Levels of Information Detail
I. Preparing a workbench	(Topic)
A. Tools	(Subtopic)
1. Screwdrivers	(Supporting detail)
a. Phillips head	(Specific example)

I.
 A.
 B.
II.
 A.
 B.
 C.
 D.
  1.
  2.
  3.
 E.
III.
 A.
 B.

  Students should question whether the composition is balanced. This outline conforms to the consistency rule of no I without a II, but clearly the amount of elaboration or development in section II far outweighs the detail in sections I and III. And within section II, subsection D is developed more than the other subsections. Seeing an outline as out of balance as this one should lead students to examine closely the information in the draft. Is there unnecessary elaboration in section II? Did the writer ramble? Or should sections I and III contain more detail? Are important pieces of information missing? Likely, adding and subtracting detail will be necessary to achieve balance.

  Outlining a written draft helps make order, consistency, and balance problems visible. Visual learners will appreciate this technique when the outline is written out. Auditory learners will benefit particularly, after writing, from reading the sentences aloud, first as they are, then as they are revised. Does the information flow logically? Listen for transition words and sensory details. Do the words evoke appropriate images? Auditory and visual learners can check one another using their preferred learning styles.

  Kinesthetic learners will find it easer to revise a draft based on its outline if the outline is created using separate strips or sheets of paper or index cards, one for each level of information or even each sentence. These cards can be reordered. Extraneous information can be sorted out and those cards removed. New cards can be written for details that should be added to the text.

  Students who have previously had negative experiences with outlining sometimes ask, Why should I outline my draft? Here are four reasons:

1. It is difficult to put into a plan of organization, whether a list or a graphic organizer or a preliminary outline, everything that should be included in a composition. As most writers create a draft, new ideas occur to them. These new ideas can be valuable. If a writer sticks rigidly to a plan, good ideas can be lost. Using an outline as a revision strategy ensures that the writer can remain spontaneous during the drafting process and still bring order to the final draft.

2. Outlining an early draft of a composition allows a writer to dig into his or her work, spot overwritten material and omissions, and adjust the text so that it is balanced and complete.

3. If it is easy to outline a draft, then the text probably is well organized. On the other hand, if there are sentences or other elements that do not fit well in a formal outline, that probably means they are misplaced or unnecessary.

4. Outlining a draft is a good way to practice a convention of effective organization. Understanding the nature of a formal outline likely will be required at some point in a student's education, and outlining to revise is an effective way to learn and to practice this skill.

SAMPLE LESSON 6.1: OUTLINING TO REVISE—AND REVISING

To pull together the strategies described in this chapter on patterns and rhythms, this lesson asks students to focus on outlining to revise and using the other strategies within this context.

Background: Following is a student composition in response to a prompt to compare and contrast two shopping malls. Other draft texts may be chosen, of course, following procedures that I have previously described.

Two Shopping Malls

A fast forty-five minutes away from where I live is a large shopping mall called Northridge. Only 10 minutes away from my house is a small shopping mall called Memorial. Both attract many shoppers, but their stores are very different.

Northridge Mall is gigantic. The Limited, The Gap, and All-Cotton are three of its many clothing stores. The stores at Northridge offer many different brands of clothing to choose from. Memorial Mall is not as big as Northridge. Brooks, Fast Foot, and Maurices are the only clothing stores I enjoy. The styles, colors, and brand names are basically all the same at Memorial.

Northridge is a modern mall. It has stores, entertainment, and restaurants to please everyone. Shoppers can be busy for hours there. Memorial Mall is old. There is not much to look at and not much to do there. After a couple of hours of shopping I am bored and ready to go home.

Northridge is the better mall by far, but it takes longer to get there. The trip is worth it when I really want to shop. Memorial is not as exciting, but it is close by and useful for everyday shopping.

Assignment: First, students should outline the sample draft. In the beginning, teachers may want to complete the outline as a whole-class process. This procedure can be especially helpful while students are learning how to outline, as it prevents individual students from creating outlines that do not correctly reflect the draft.

Once the outline has been made, the teacher should ask students to answer the following analysis questions. Depending on the grade level and revision experience of the students, this procedure may be done by students working in pairs or triads or as a whole-class process.

1. Is the information in the outline in logical order? Does section II reasonably follow I, B follow A, and so on? Check the pattern of organization by identifying key ideas and transition words. Read the draft aloud from the outline and listen for rhythms that indicate effective sequencing. What adjustments need to be made in the order of ideas or the use of transition words?

2. Are the ideas or topics sufficiently developed? Was it possible to list subcategories 1 and 2 (maybe even subheads a and b) that elaborate on the topic stated in the A and B level? Does more detail need to be incorporated? Consider using sensory reportage and creating kinesthetic imagery.

3. Is the draft balanced according to the outline? Are there about as many supporting details for A as there are for B and C, and so forth? Does some information not seem to fit anywhere in the outline? Should that information be developed or discarded?

4. Are there holes in the draft, places where information seems to be missing? What new information is needed, and how should it be incorporated into the revised draft?

Assessment: The teacher should ask students to develop a revised draft based on their answers to these analysis questions. Again, this work can be done as a whole-class process, or pairs or triads of students can develop group drafts that then can be shared, and the teacher can lead a discussion comparing various groups' approaches to the revision.

Like the other sample lessons, this one is intended to illustrate strategies that should be introduced and practiced multiple times. Some of the activities are quick and easy to accomplish; others will need to be undertaken over several days or class periods. This sample lesson portrays a relatively complete process, but the various activities can be done separately at first in order to help students internalize the goals and procedures.

The more that students work with these strategies, the more comfortable they will become with talking about how they think about writing and using the planning, drafting, and revising processes independently. Visual, auditory, and kinesthetic learners will gain experience working in their own learning style but also in other styles, thereby increasing their repertoire of successful writing strategies.

SAMPLE LESSON 6.2: PATTERNS AND RHYTHMS FOR WRITING SENSE

This lesson asks students to focus on outlining to revise and to use the other strategies related to using patterns and rhythms to strengthen their writing.

Background: The following is a student draft written in response to a prompt to recount an exciting experience.

Riding the Space Whip

The Space Whip was a high ride. On top of it you might be 30 or 40 feet off the ground. People sit two to a cage.

I went to the carnival with my friend Terry. Terry talked me into going on the highest ride in the park.

The cages turn around at the end of long arms. The arms rotate like the spokes of a wheel, except that they are only connected in the center. Each cage came slowly around and stopped at the ground to let people get in and out. When the ride was in motion, the spokes whirled, and the cages whipped around on the ends of the spokes.

The Space Whip looked like a futuristic windmill. I'm a little scared of heights. When the cage stopped in front of Terry and me, my heart jumped into my throat. I was sure the Space Whip would scare me to death.

Assignment: Students should first outline the sample draft. This can be done as a whole-class process, or students can work individually or in pairs or triads. Once the outline has been made, the teacher should ask students to answer the following analysis questions:

1. Is the information in the outline in logical order? Does section II reasonably follow I, B follow A, and so on? Check the pattern of organization by identifying key ideas and transition words. Read the draft aloud from the outline and listen for rhythms that indicate effective sequencing. What adjustments need to be made in the order of ideas or the use of transition words?

2. Are the ideas or topics sufficiently developed? Was it possible to list subheads 1 and 2 (maybe even subheads a and b) that elaborate on the topic stated in the A and B level? Does more detail need to be incorporated? Consider using sensory reportage and creating kinesthetic imagery.

3. Is the draft balanced according to the outline? Are there about as many supporting details for A as there are for B and C, and so forth? Is there extraneous information that does not seem to fit anywhere in the outline? Should that information be developed or discarded?

4. Are there holes in the draft, places where information seems to be missing? What new information is needed, and how should it be incorporated into the revised draft?

Assessment: The teacher should ask students to develop a revised draft on the basis of their answers to these analysis questions. The revision also can be done as a whole-class activity, or students can develop individual or small-group revised drafts. Then the teacher can lead a discussion comparing the approaches of various groups to the revision.

7 Choosing the Right Words

M any writers work most effectively when they take an idea (or an assignment or a test prompt) and make a plan (mental, written, graphic, or other) and then create a draft *before* giving attention to details. These details can include matters such as ensuring coherence, using appropriate transitional language, adding needed information (fleshing out), and other elements best addressed during revision. An important lesson for all students, not just visual, auditory, and kinesthetic learners, is that drafting is only the beginning. Real writing is revising. One important element to address during revision is word choice.

As the Roman philosopher Seneca, who lived from 4 B.C. to A.D. 65, said, "What is required is not a lot words, but effectual ones." His advice is still sound nearly two millennia later. Words are the building blocks of meaning, and well-chosen words convey meaning most clearly. During the drafting process, when students are working to get an idea down on paper, the first words that come to mind will suffice. During the revision process, students need to examine their words carefully and make adjustments to ensure that their meaning is clear.

BASIC WORDS: NOUNS AND VERBS

Using precise words allows a writer to convey meaning clearly and succinctly. Nouns and verbs, using the traditional grammatical terms, are basic building blocks and so make a good starting point for study. One exercise for noun recognition is to ask for students' impressions about the meaning of the word *building*. The teacher might begin by saying, "Please write down a sentence or two describing what you think I mean when

I say the word *building*." Students' responses likely will range widely: "a structure with rooms ... maybe offices ... like the school ... could be a house or a factory or a store," and so on. It should become evident as the students share their written responses aloud that building can mean many different types of structure.

This is a good time to introduce students to the concepts of *denotation* and *connotation*. The denotative, or the most specific, direct meaning, of building is similar to the dictionary definition: A building is a structure, usually for human habitation as a residence or workplace.

Connotation refers to the associations suggested by a word, its attributes of meaning in addition to the literal meaning. Effective writers look beyond choosing words by their denotation to choosing those whose specific connotations are closest to the meaning they are seeking to convey. The word *building* has too many possible connotations for a reader to see what the writer has in mind without further explanation.

Let us say that the building in this example is a house. The teacher might repeat the previous exercise, saying, "Please write down a sentence or two describing what you think I mean when I say the word *house*." Again, the responses will likely express a range of connotations. Next the teacher might ask, "What are some more precise nouns—synonyms—for house that suggest specific house connotations?"

Students can brainstorm as a whole class or in small groups to generate a list of house synonyms, or this can be a teachable moment to introduce the use of a thesaurus. In either case, the students should be able to come up with some of the following:

- residence
- domicile
- dwelling
- shelter
- mansion
- shack
- hovel
- town house

Students can share the connotations of these and other words in writing or verbally. Visual and kinesthetic learners may grasp the concept of connotation better by finding visual examples, such as photographs from magazines, and clipping out images that show the meanings. The words and illustrative clippings can be displayed on posters created by individual students or small groups. And the posters then can serve as visual reminders while students are writing.

Verbs can be treated in a similar fashion. In fact, a sample paragraph from Chapter 6 provides an example that can be used to show students a variety of verbs that convey more precise meanings of how a horse moves:

> Horsemanship competition is simply doing things with the horse to show how well you have control over the horse. At first, I rode at a walking pace. Holding my horse to a *walk* at about 2 miles per hour was not easy. And it also was hard to let the horse gradually speed up. Next, I rode at a *jog*, which was just a little faster, about 4 miles per hour. My horse wanted to go faster, but I kept control. Then, I rode at a *trot.* A trotting horse is going about 6 miles per hour, which is a pretty comfortable speed. Finally, I rode at a *lope,* an easy 8 miles per hour, which is a fast, open speed for my horse but still much slower than a full-out *gallop.*

Walk, jog, trot, lope, and *gallop* produce more specific mental images in a reader's mind than simply *move.*

Another point teachers should make is that poor writers resort to using adjectives and adverbs to help out weak nouns and verbs. Effective writers find strong nouns and verbs and eliminate the use of helper words. This is not to say that adjectives and adverbs should not be used at all. They should be used to enrich clear meaning, rather than prop up weak word choices. A way to teach this concept is to give students examples of weak adjective-noun and verb-adverb constructions and ask them to find more effective one-word alternatives. Here are some examples:

Adjective-noun example: The *fast car* drove quickly around the corner.

Possible alternatives: *racer, roadster, speedster*

Verb-adverb example: The red car *drove quickly* around the corner.

Possible alternatives: *raced, sped, roared*

CORRECT AND POLITICALLY CORRECT

Another aspect of effective word choice is determining the correct word. There is nothing essentially wrong about a writer using the words *small house* instead of choosing a more descriptive noun, such as cottage or bungalow. On the other hand, it is wrong if a writer uses *disinterested* (meaning impartial) when the word needed is *uninterested* (meaning simply not interested).

For visual, auditory, and kinesthetic learners, as for all learners, consistently reading well-written prose is an invaluable aid to fine-tuning their eyes and ears to correct language use. General reading and reading specifically focused on word choice and correctness can be supplemented by dictionary and thesaurus exercises. Get-up-and-go-find activities are motivating and engaging for visual, auditory, and kinesthetic learners.

Most language arts texts include lists of easily confused or misused words—word devils or word demons—that can be the basis for interesting and thought-provoking discussions and exercises that engage student writers in discovering the value of basic resources. If a useful collection of these words is not at hand, teachers can do an Internet search—on a key phrase such as *easily confused words*, for example. As a point of reference, Figure 7.1 shows several sets of frequently confused words.

Visual learners need to have troublesome words pointed out and see them used correctly. The corresponding activity for auditory learners is

Figure 7.1	Words Easily Confused		
comprise	compose		
alternate	alternative		
save	spare		
anniversary	birthday		
rob	steal		
stationery	stationary		
stranger	foreigner		
emigrant	immigrant		
allusion	illusion		
farther	further		
few	less		
disinterested	uninterested		
passed	past		
precede	proceed		
tasteful	tasty		
currently	presently		
affect	effect		
cancel	postpone		
noise	sound		
memory	souvenir		
complement	compliment		
principal	principle		
desert	dessert		
receipt	recipe		
elder	older	elderly	
their	there	they're	
cite	site	sight	
borrow	lend	loan	
lie	lay	lain	laid
council	councilor	counsel	counselor

reading aloud so that they can say and hear these words used correctly. And kinesthetic learners can act out correct meanings in some cases or manipulate the words physically, such as by using posters, paper strips, or other objects—activities that involve moving. For example, writers sometimes confuse the words *compose* and *comprise,* the first set of words in Figure 7.1. The teacher might display the sentence, Fifty states comprise the United States, and ask, "Is the word *comprise* used correctly this sentence? See what the dictionary has to say."

Students will find that the traditional answer is that this usage is incorrect. The rule is that a whole comprises the parts; the parts compose the whole. Therefore, to be correct, a sentence should read, Fifty states compose the United States or The United States comprises fifty states.

This example, as it happens, also provides an excellent basis for discussing how language changes. English (and all modern languages) are alive; words, meanings, and usage change over time. The compilers of *The American Heritage Dictionary of the English Language* (4th ed., 2000) point out the following regarding the traditional rule about comprise and compose:

> Even though careful writers often maintain this distinction, *comprise* is increasingly used in place of *compose,* especially in the passive: *The Union is comprised of 50 states.* Our surveys show that opposition to this usage is abating. In the late 1960s, 53 percent of the Usage Panel found this usage unacceptable; in 1996, only 35 percent objected. (p. 379, at *comprise*) [italics added]

Some students may find the study of language changes interesting and helpful for understanding today's usage and for understanding why some people use words in ways that now are seen as old-fashioned or incorrect. For example, nowadays we take for granted the correct pronunciation of *cooperation,* that the *coop* is not pronounced like the *coop* in *chicken coop* but as *co* with a long *o* and *op* with a short *o.* But that was not always the case. When the word first came into use, it was spelled with a hyphen: *co-operation.* The hyphen helped readers over the change from a long *o* in *co* to a short *o* in *operation.* The word then went through a hyphenless stage with an umlaut on the second *o* to distinguish the different sounds of the two os: *coöperation.* Finally, the word became so familiar that the visual cues to pronunciation were discarded.

Another example is the word *bus,* which began as *omnibus* when these vehicles were first used in the late 19th and early 20th centuries. The use of *bus* in books of the early 1900s show the word with an apostrophe—*'bus*—to indicate the missing *omni.* The late John Ciardi, a poet and etymologist, wrote three delightfully accessible books about word histories that middle and high school students may find fascinating: *A Browser's*

Dictionary, A Second Browser's Dictionary, and *A Third Browser's Dictionary*. All three were reissued in paperback in 2001.

The idea that language is alive also affects the choice of words that are correct according to current societal norms, and those words are often called politically correct. For example, before the civil rights movement, black people were referred to as colored, a use no longer considered appropriate (though retained by the NAACP, the National Association for the Advancement of Colored People, which was founded in 1909, when the term was commonplace). The term *people of color* is preferred today. Similarly, the word *Negro* generally fell by the wayside, first replaced by the term *Afro-American* and now more commonly by *African American*. The women's rights movement increased sensitivity to sexism in language. Feminists objected to the dominance of male terminology, for example, as seen in *man* (in the universal sense) and *mankind*. *Humans* or *people* and *humankind* are now viewed as more politically correct choices. In the same way, stereotypical assumptions about the roles of both sexes are no longer correct. Secretaries, for example, should not be assumed to be women, nor should business executives be assumed to be men. A useful class discussion can come from brainstorming other examples, such as gender-specific words— *policeman, mailman, fireman, congressman*—and words that carry traditional sexist connotations, such as *secretary, nanny, teacher, principal,* and so on. Students can then work on identifying nonsexist equivalents.

Sentences from works published before the mid-20th century can be sampled for student practice in identifying outdated, racist, or sexist words and correcting the usage. For example, the teacher might ask, "What assumptions are being made in the following sentences? How should we revise the sentences for today's usage?" Consider the following, for example:

A nurse must be alert to sudden changes in a patient's condition. *She* must monitor pulse and temperature at regular intervals.

Clearly the assumption is that nurses are female. But there have always been male nurses, even when the nursing profession was considered to be mainly women's work. The opposite has been true for doctors. Once the profession was almost exclusively male, but now there are many female doctors.

One way to reform the sentence to nonsexist language is to use the plural:

Nurses must be alert to sudden changes in a patient's condition. *They* must monitor pulse and temperature at regular intervals.

Another way to improve it is to retain the singular noun and to use both male and female pronouns:

A nurse must be alert to sudden changes in a patient's condition. *He or she* must monitor pulse and temperature at regular intervals.

He or she or *she or he* is preferred over the occasionally used, shorthand construction *s/he*, which is impossible to read aloud correctly, as any auditory learner will quickly point out. Of course, if *he or she* is used too frequently, better alternatives are to use the plural or simply to reconstruct the sentences to avoid the pronouns by using a participle, as in:

Nurses must be alert to sudden changes in a patient's condition, monitoring pulse and temperature at regular intervals.

Activities and discussions that involve manipulating words and sentence structures increase students' versatility as writers. Physically rearranging sentences, trying various words, moving from page to dictionary to thesaurus—all of these activities are well suited to kinesthetic learners because the activities require movement and action. Visual learners need many of the same activities so that they clearly see how correct words replace incorrect choices and how sentences can be revised to clarify meaning. And auditory learners will benefit from saying words and sentences aloud, verbalizing the problems and their solutions. Auditory learners are the real beneficiaries of small-group and whole-class discussions of these matters.

MORE BASIC WORDS: ADJECTIVES AND ADVERBS

The more that teachers and students play with words in instructional contexts, the more exciting it becomes for students to seek out effective words and to pay attention to making the best choices in their writing.

Earlier the discussion focused on choosing descriptive nouns and verbs, words that convey precise meanings without the need of helper words. But adjectives and adverbs do have a place in writing, provided they are not overused or misused. They should amplify effective nouns and verbs, not prop up weak ones. For example, the noun *mansion* produces a more specific mental image than does the word *house*. But mansion by itself still conveys only a partial picture. The teacher might ask students to brainstorm adjectives that modify (or amplify) the mental images that readers are likely to construct and then to explain those images in greater detail. Following are a few sample adjective-noun pairs:

- decaying mansion
- restored mansion
- hulking mansion

- resplendent mansion
- sprawling mansion

Each of these adjectives adds to the mental image that the reader is likely to construct of the mansion.

The same kind of exercise can be used to discuss and manipulate adverbs. For example, the verb *dashed* conveys a more specific image than does, say, *ran quickly*. But how did the runner dash? Here are a few verb-adverb pairs:

- dashed awkwardly
- dashed impetuously
- dashed nimbly
- dashed angrily
- dashed eagerly

An interesting way to involve visual, auditory, and kinesthetic learning is to ask three students to "perform" a group of these word pairs. For example, the triad might take on the examples above in this way. One student would make a card showing a word pair (such as *dashed awkwardly*). The second student would say the words aloud in the presentation as the first student shows the card. The third student would demonstrate dashing awkwardly. Students from the middle grades into high school enjoy this activity, and it puts the spotlight on appropriate word use in an engaging, lighthearted way.

A useful follow-up to this type of wordplay is using the word pairs meaningfully in a piece of writing. Students can work together in pairs or small groups to create a draft. Here is one example:

Last weekend my friend Missy and I went with my mom on a home tour. One house we read about ahead of time was the Johnson mansion. After the last member of the Johnson family died, the home fell into decay. Now, the brochure said, it had been renovated. When we rounded a corner and saw the *restored mansion*, Missy was so impressed that she *dashed impetuously* up the front sidewalk to get a closer look.

A follow-up exercise of this type extends the word-focused lesson into drafting and later revising a piece of writing.

Another way to enlarge the study of effective nouns, verbs, adjectives, and adverbs is to use the sense exploration template (Figure 3.2). A completed template from a previous lesson can make a good starting point.

The teacher might say, "Look closely at the sensory reportage terms that you placed in the five columns of your template. Now that we have talked about using strong nouns, adjectives, verbs, and adverbs, do some of your descriptive words seem weak or strong in the mental images they create? What might be some alternatives to the weak descriptions?"

BREVITY

In *Hamlet,* Polonius says that "brevity is the soul of wit." Choosing words that express the writer's meaning clearly and concisely also is at the heart of effective writing. Students sometimes go the long way on the path to meaning because they have read and heard overblown phrases used by others. Helping students spot wordiness in writing samples can help them eliminate it in their own writing.

As in the case of other word-choice exercises, visual, auditory, and kinesthetic learners will be better able to grasp the concept of brevity if the teacher uses a hands-on approach. For example, the teacher might ask students to use butcher paper to copy the following paragraph and then to read it aloud:

> The two scientists on the expedition were in the neighborhood of a volcano when they noticed that the air was becoming increasingly smoky. One scientist said to the other, "In the event that we hear rumbling from underground, we probably should run." The other replied, "I think we might hear that rumbling in the near future."

Next, the teacher would hand out slips of paper, each with one of the following words written on it. The teacher might then ask, "Can you cross out some groups of words in this paragraph and replace them with one of the words on these slips of paper?"

near

if

soon

The resulting revision might look like this:

> The two scientists on the expedition were ~~in the neighborhood of~~ *near* a volcano when they noticed that the air was becoming increasingly smoky. One scientist said to the other, "~~In the event~~

~~that~~ *If* we hear rumbling from underground, we probably should run." The other replied, "I think we might hear that rumbling ~~in the near future~~ *soon*."

Redundant phrases are a related problem. For example, a pet phrase of some educators is *forward progress.* But is not progress always forward? Otherwise, it would be regress. The solution to this redundancy is simply to use *progress* by itself. How often do we hear *at this point in time* when either *at this time* or *at this point* would suffice? Students see and hear these redundant phrases and incorporate them into their writing. Teachers can sensitize students to these problematic word choices and teach them to be brief.

Figure 7.2 shows some other wordy or redundant phrases that can be replaced to achieve brevity. Students might be asked to find or think of others.

Finally, another word-choice topic related to brevity is what might be termed *shortcut slang.* Examples include *kinda, sorta, lotsa,* and other collapsed words that are becoming commonplace in certain usage but are still considered inappropriate in anything more than entirely personal communications, such as letters and e-mail. Students cannot be expected to understand the distinction offhand. *Kinda* is all right in e-mail to a friend, but it should be *kind of* when used in school work, test compositions, or adult writing situations. Such words often have special appeal to visual, auditory, and kinesthetic learners. The words look all right (students read them in fiction and see them in the comics), they sound natural, and they are quick and easy to write or to keyboard. E-mail and Internet messaging have given rise to a new collection of shortcut slang, such as *u r* for *you are* and *prolly* for *probably.* When such constructions creep into written assignments, they should be treated as word-choice matters and corrected accordingly.

Figure 7.2 Wordy Phrases and Brief Alternatives

in the neighborhood of	near
along the lines of	like
in the event that	if
in view of the fact	because
in the near future	soon
repeat again	repeat
forward progress	progress
close proximity	near
advance planning	planning
necessary requirement	requirement

SPELLING IMPROVEMENT

A few words about spelling are in order. Almost all children, adolescents, and even adult writers, when they are intent on writing, will make up their own spellings of words they do not know how to spell from memory. This is a useful strategy. In fact, too much concentration on correct spelling during the drafting stage inhibits creativity and impedes fluency. But hastily misspelled words should be seen as placeholders and not ignored during revision and editing.

Additionally, young people tend to learn correct spellings naturally over time as they are exposed to readings in which words appear that they want to use in their own writing. Consequently, teachers should not be too demanding in the early years with regard to proper spelling of all words in students' writing.

On the other hand, there are times when correctness can and should be expected. For example, when students use common words or words specifically related to information under study, misspellings should be noted for correction during revision. Teachers or peer readers can circle spelling errors so that students can look up the correct spellings and make changes.

There are about as many ways to teach spelling as there are flavors of ice cream. The ones that work best for visual, auditory, and kinesthetic learners naturally involve seeing, saying, and doing. The following are steps that may be useful directions for students:

Write the word.

Spell the word as you write it.

Say the word.

Make up a sentence and say it aloud.

Write the sentence down and read it aloud.

Act out the word or the sentence.

This set of activities can be used for set lists, such as commonly misspelled words. Another strategy is for the student to create a personal spelling list, including words he or she has misspelled in recent written work. And yet another strategy is to draw words from a subject under study, such as terms related to the kind of math problems students are tackling. Many textbooks provide lists of important words used in the various chapters. In every case, just asking students to learn how to spell these words is an ineffective instructional strategy. Teachers will help students achieve greater success by teaching them techniques for studying the words that draw on their individual learning styles.

There seems to be general agreement among the experts that studying lists of words is a more effective instructional approach than studying spelling serendipitously, word by word. Lists can be as short as four or five words or as long as 20 or 30, but that tends to be the reasonable range. Shorter lists for younger students, longer lists for older students is a good rule of thumb.

SAMPLE LESSON 7.1: REVIEWING THE WORDS

The sample lesson that follows is an attempt to touch on the various right-word themes in this chapter.

Background. The following is a student response to the prompt: Write a brief review of a concert you recently attended.

East High School Concert

I thought the concert was pretty good. Some of their singing was good, even though one of their song were little flat. They were well organized. Most of there songs I could see the picture in my mind when they were singing. One of there songs were kinda sad. I could really since that kind of feeling.

There were some classical that I really enjoyed. I always think of classical I think it is dumb because its always slow. But in these classical music there was something in it that I really enjoyed. I don't know what it is. I gussed not all the classical music are dumb.

There were some up beat that will put you into motion. You will feel like you could just dance with the music. Most of all the music I heard, I liked the up beat music because I like fast moving music.

Assignment. Students should examine this draft concert review carefully and answer the following questions about word choice:

1. Does the writer use effective nouns and verbs? Choose two ineffective nouns and two ineffective verbs and suggest alternatives for each of them.

2. Does the writer use any incorrect word choices (not misspellings)? Choose two or three examples and suggest correct alternatives.

3. Does the writer use effective adjectives and adverbs? Choose two examples of ineffective adjectives or adverbs and suggest alternatives for them.

4. Does the writer misspell any words? Choose two or three examples and show how the words should be spelled correctly.

The follow-up to this assignment is to ask students to share their responses, perhaps first in pairs or triads and then with the whole class. Showing the corrections, reading them aloud, and having students write and correct on chart paper engage visual, auditory, and kinesthetic learners in seeing, saying, and doing.

This lesson can be extended by using strategies from the other chapters to revise the draft more completely, looking at organization, sentence structure, details and development, and so on.

SAMPLE LESSON 7.2:
UP CLOSE—CHOOSING THE RIGHT WORDS

This lesson touches on several right-word themes from this chapter.

Background. Following is a student response to a prompt calling for the student to relate a personal experience connected in some way to history.

The Old Graveyard

One day I went on a camping trip with my family. Late in the afternoon, my dad and I went for a long bike ride. We were following an overgrown foot trail. We stopped by a pond and started looking around and exploring the area. My dad spotted a path that was barly visible in the tall grass and weeds. We decided to follow the path and see where it would lead. It was hard to get through the trail because of the weeds and bushes scratching our legs.

Finally, we got to a clearing and the first thing I saw was a big ole white stone sticking out of the ground. It was then that I knew that we had come upon an old graveyard. We walked over to the gravestones and tried reading the words. They were difficult to read because of the age of the stones. I could make out some of the dates though, and they were from the 1800s and early 1900s. I was amazed and excited to be around such old tombstones.

A couple of years later we came back to this small family graveyard. At this time I explored the area even more. I went deeper into the woods and found two graves from the Civil war period. Another grave I found had a cement lamb on top of the gravestone. I read the words and dates on this stone. It was the gravestone of an eight-year-old boy who died in the early 1900s. I felt really bad for someone who died so young.

Coming across this graveyard made me think about my life because I wondered where I will be buried when I die. Will people come and look at my grave and wonder how old and long ago it was when I died? This discovery really helped me to change the way I think. Will anyone remember me in the future, or will I be forgotten like these lost gravestones?

Assignment. Students should examine this draft carefully and answer the following questions about word choice:

1. Does the writer use effective nouns and verbs? Choose two ineffective nouns and two ineffective verbs and suggest alternatives for each of them.

2. Does the writer use any incorrect word choices (not misspellings)? Choose two or three examples and suggest correct alternatives.

3. Does the writer use effective adjectives and adverbs? Choose two examples of ineffective adjectives or adverbs and suggest alternatives for them.

4. Does the writer misspell any words? Choose two or three examples and show how the words should be spelled correctly.

The follow-up to this assignment is to ask students to share their responses, perhaps first in pairs or triads and then with the whole class. Showing the corrections, reading them aloud, and having students write and correct on chart paper engage visual, auditory, and kinesthetic learners in seeing, saying, and doing. This lesson also can be extended by using strategies from the other chapters to revise the draft more completely, looking at organization, sentence structure, details and development, and so on.

REFERENCES

Ciardi, J. (1980). *A browser's dictionary.* New York: HarperCollins.

Ciardi, J. (1983). *A second browser's dictionary.* New York: HarperCollins.

Ciardi, J. (1985). *A third browser's dictionary.* New York: HarperCollins. (Each edition of *The Browser's Dictionary* was reissued in a *Common Reader* edition by Akadine, Pleasantville, NY, in 2001)

The American heritage dictionary of the English language (4th ed.). (2000). Boston: Houghton Mifflin.

8 Increasing Focused Engagement

At the start of this book I suggested that many people, including teachers, hold two major misconceptions about writing. These misconceptions are that writing is a deliberate, linear process and that students should be taught to write in a deliberate, linear manner. Teachers who teach based on these misconceptions wonder why not all of their students become effective writers. Often, the students most challenged to learn in this way are visual, auditory, and kinesthetic learners.

The simple fact is that no one-size-fits-all model exists for effective writing instruction. The writing process is indeed a collection of processes. Thus, to attempt in good faith to teach all students, a teacher must adopt a multidimensional view of how writing happens and teach accordingly. Adopting this point of view is especially important in order to reach and teach visual, auditory, and kinesthetic learners.

In the preceding chapters I have endeavored to describe specific strategies that teachers can use to engage visual, auditory, and kinesthetic learners. Many of these strategies are useful for enlarging the writing repertoires of all students, regardless of their preferred learning style. This final chapter is devoted to teaching strategies that work in concert with the other strategies in order to increase focused engagement in the various acts of composing.

I attempt to answer three questions in this chapter:

- How can teachers help student writers focus on specific writing improvements?

- What techniques will assist students in pinpointing their learning needs?
- How can teachers avoid reading/marking/correcting overload—and student feedback overload?

It makes sense to begin with a basic principle: Focus is selective. An object is in sharp focus or blurry depending on whether it is the object of attention or merely part of the surroundings. In helping students learn to write well, the teacher will get the best results by focusing on selected objects in a systematic way and not on attempting to see and do everything at once.

SELECTIVE CORRECTION

Teachers of writing sometimes believe—or are pressured to believe—that correcting a student's writing means marking every error. At an advanced level, when errors are likely to be few, this instructional strategy can be reasonable in some circumstances. But for most students in elementary, middle, and high school it is almost always self-defeating. The student whose paper "bleeds" red ink likely will feel overwhelmed rather than empowered. For visual, auditory, and kinesthetic learners—the students who often are most challenged to write well—comprehensive correction amounts to overcorrection. Many students whose papers drown in a sea of red simply give up, or they miss the real point of the lesson (if there is one), or they try to fix everything and end up fragmenting their efforts.

Why do many teachers feel compelled to correct every error? Some teachers feel as though they have an obligation to the student to point out all errors in the belief that doing so will lead the student to correct them. This may or may not be the case. It usually will not happen with the poorest writers. Some teachers feel pressured by parents or administrators who view uncorrected student errors as a sign of shoddy teaching. The teacher should understand that the goal of reading and marking student work is not merely to point out errors but to help students improve their writing, something that takes a guiding hand rather than a pointing finger.

Selective correction means just that: selecting what to correct and what to ignore in a student's writing, based on the goal of the lesson. The following are steps a teacher can use to implement selective correction as an instructional strategy:

1. The teacher decides on one or two focal points, or targets, prior to correcting a writing assignment. On general assignments, for example, the teacher might mark only capitalization and punctuation errors. On

another, only grammatical errors. And so on. In each case a target or limited set of characteristics would be designated for concentration. For writing based on a particular focus, such as transition words, just that element would be marked.

2. The teacher writes a target notation (capitalization, run-on sentences, transition words, and so on) in the upper left-hand corner of the student's paper to let the student—and his or her parents—know what the focus of the lesson is and what type of errors have been marked. Later, students and the teacher also can use this target notation as a sorting key when reviewing a portfolio of the student's writing. (Portfolios are discussed in the next section.)

3. When returning the students' papers, the teacher discusses the target notation and re-teaches those skills in which students are deficient. Teachers cannot assume that marking errors equals teaching. Students often need direct instruction in order to correct their errors. This correction/instruction phase also is an opportunity for students to work cooperatively as an extension of prior collaborative writing and editing.

Selective correction should not be limited to the mechanics of language. Teachers can mark student writing using marginal comments for more complex considerations, such as clarity, organization, and development. But the focus still should be limited and a target notation recorded. A teacher's priorities tell students what is really important, and that applies equally to simple and to complex concepts. Selective correction helps the teacher avoid marking only simple (and often numerous) errors and ignoring more important concepts. Grammar, spelling, and punctuation should not be allowed to become the hobgoblins of students' writing endeavors.

The target notation also gives teachers a way of accounting for all the skills and writing principles they teach. In this way, over time, they can ensure that everything that needs to be taught has been taught and that emphasis has been given where it has been needed.

Parents, administrators, and sometimes other teachers may question the use of selective correction because it departs from the mark-every-error approach with which they are familiar. Teachers might worry, "Won't marking just some errors mislead students? How will students improve if their mistakes are not pointed out to them?" As they introduce the use of selective correction to students, they also need to be aware that parents, administrators, and their colleagues may need to be briefed about why selective correction makes more sense than comprehensive correction for students struggling to learn how to write well. The following are six points that teachers can make:

1. Marking every error discourages young and struggling writers. Students should be expected to make errors as they learn and practice.

2. Marking every error often gives students too much to deal with at one time. They may not be able to winnow serious errors from trivial ones or to improve on their own.

3. Because selective correction focuses on target characteristics, teachers are able to concentrate instruction on specifics. If teachers use the targeted corrections as starting points for direct teaching, students are more likely to develop the writing skills they need to avoid making the same mistakes in the future.

4. By choosing different targets for different assignments, teachers can ensure that all of the skills that need to be taught are taught—but in bite-size pieces that are easier for students to understand and incorporate into their writing practice.

5. The target notation written at the top of each paper indicates to students and parents the types of errors being marked and serves notice that selective correction is being used. This makes clear to students and their parents that the teacher has not merely missed other errors.

6. A distinction must be made between marking errors and grading. Marking errors, whether done by the writer, a peer editor, or the teacher, is designed to help students recognize and correct writing problems. Grades evaluate the final product.

Selective correction is an effective technique not only for students in all grades and in all disciplines but for busy teachers as well, because it is a more efficient use of their time. Obviously, it takes less time to mark only one or two types of error in a paper than it does to mark them all. But selective correction does more than that; it is a quick, direct diagnostic because it targets the need for follow-up teaching. And if it shows that most students have mastered a certain skill, the teacher can focus on other skills and structure further instruction (extra help or peer tutoring) as needed.

Teachers who use selective correction will find that they spend less time marking papers and can require more writing assignments from students. In this way students gain more practice at writing, and practice is necessary for learning to write well.

THE IMPORTANCE OF PORTFOLIOS

A portfolio is basically a collection of a student's work, but there are many types of them. A comprehensive portfolio might include, or attempt to include, every product the student produces, from tests and worksheets to graphic organizers, rough drafts, and finished written work. A focused writing portfolio might limit the contents to writing-related materials, including visual organizers, audiotapes, videotapes, drafts, and finished papers. A cross-disciplinary writing portfolio might include the same kind of materials as the focused writing portfolio but gather from all of the student's classes.

For the purpose of enhancing writing instruction, the type that seems to work best for visual, auditory, and kinesthetic learners is the focused writing portfolio. It helps the student focus on writing without being distracted by other materials, such as worksheets, quizzes, tests, and other papers. If the school has a comprehensive and well-coordinated writing-across-the-disciplines program, a cross-disciplinary writing portfolio can be a step up, but such programs tend to be rare, especially at the middle and high school levels.

In working with visual, auditory, and kinesthetic learners, it also is important to think in practical storage terms. Not everything in the portfolio will or should be paper. And so the idea of a portfolio being essentially a folder of some kind is inadequate. A better option for individual portfolios is sturdy storage boxes large enough to accommodate audiotapes and videotapes, for example, but small enough to be stored in the classroom or transported by the student. Storage boxes in several bookshelf sizes are readily available in office supply stores.

Following are examples of artifacts that might be included in a student's writing portfolio:

- Class notes, writing ideas, lesson handouts
- Planning materials, such as outlines, lists, visual organizers
- Research information, photocopies, online printouts
- Recorded work-in-progress audiotapes or videotapes
- Drafts, rubrics, critiques
- Finished papers

Portfolios are not intended to be static collections. They should be viewed as dynamic and interactive. The following are some possibilities for organizing and using portfolio contents:

Project focus. Students gather all of the artifacts of each extended writing project, from initial jottings about ideas, research materials, organizers (visual, auditory, kinesthetic), drafts, rubrics, and reviews and critiques to the final product. These materials form the process record of a given writing project that students and teachers subsequently can analyze individually or together—to evaluate writing strengths and weaknesses, to review and revise process components, or to seek models for future projects.

Strategy focus. Students gather all of the artifacts related to a specific writing type or technique. For example, students might collect all of the various types of visual organizers they have used and analyze the purpose and effectiveness of each with an eye to making future choices. The target notation on written drafts can be an effective organizing tool to assist students in locating related items.

Demonstration focus. Students demonstrate their competence in using various writing strategies. The effective writing teacher will be interested in more than simply the students' choice of their best finished writing, however. Students can gather examples of effective planning and drafting or examples of writing strategies they have mastered.

Presentation focus. Students choose examples of their best finished work as a culminating activity or in lieu of a final exam.

Finally, an important aspect of portfolios is their use for idea-mining. Researchers who dip repeatedly into the same data to answer various questions are said to be data-mining. Idea-mining works in the same way. Students should be encouraged to mine their portfolios to look for ideas they can develop in new ways, strategies they can use and refine, and so forth. Most professional writers keep a list of ideas so that when they find themselves casting about for something to write, they can return to that list. As students develop their portfolios, they will be able to dip into them from time to time and find good ideas that they have forgotten, strategies that they can use again or adapt, and other information that can be reused or expanded.

MAKING AND USING RUBRICS

I mentioned rubrics in the preceding section, and so I should explain what I mean. Rubrics are simple but powerful devices for isolating and thereby focusing on certain writing characteristics. They are helpful for all writers but especially for visual, auditory, and kinesthetic learners because rubrics employ an alternative visual form (a chart or a table) rather than just text to encourage discussions about writing and provide for hands-on analysis.

Figure 8.1 shows a basic rubric. In the simple chart, the objectives of the writer (or the desired characteristics of the writing) are listed in the left-hand column:

The Writer:	Some of the Time	Most of the Time	All of the Time
Figure 8.1 Basic Rubric Example			
Uses complete sentences			X
Uses more than one sense description		X	
Uses clear organization			X
Spells words correctly	X		

- Uses complete sentences
- Uses more than one sense description
- Uses clear organization
- Spells words correctly

Three indicators of quality top the columns on the right: *some of the time, most of the time, all of the time.* To use the rubric, a critical reader reads the student's paper and rates it. The purpose is analysis and feedback. Student writers gain a sense of how well they have accomplished the lesson objectives, whether they use the rubric themselves or receive it after someone else has read their work. Critical readers can include a peer, the teacher, or someone else, such as a parent, a classroom aid, or a tutor.

The real power of a rubric is felt when students work with the teacher to create the rubric from the start. As students begin to work on a piece of writing or even a plan for writing, the teacher might ask, "What should we focus on in this assignment?" The class as a group can then decide which writing objectives or characteristics they believe are most important at that stage in the writing process and for that particular assignment. These emphases are significant. Rubrics should be fluid. They should be developed for particular aspects of writing lessons and assignments, not just for the final draft. For this reason a generic rubric will soon outlive its usefulness. The process of tailoring a rubric is essential to ensuring appropriate focus.

As students engage in making rubrics as a class, they can then transfer that skill to small-group and individual use. Students can make individualized rubrics as a way of focusing on certain aspects of their writing and of guiding subsequent revision.

Teachers can take advantage of the visual and kinesthetic aspects of rubrics by translating text-based assignments into this more visual format. For example, in Chapter 6 the sample lesson involved making an outline (outlining to revise) of a short description we called "Two Shopping Malls." The assignment after making the outline was to answer four questions:

Figure 8.2   Advanced Rubric Example

The Writer:	1 Seldom	2	3	4 Usually
Has a clear purpose			X	
Uses transparent organization	X			
Uses accurate vocabulary				X
Applies correct sentence structure				X
Includes appropriate sentence variety	X			
Uses correct punctuation				X

1. Is the information in the outline in logical order?

2. Are the ideas or topics sufficiently developed?

3. Is the draft balanced according to the outline?

4. Are there holes in the draft, places where information seems to be missing?

These four questions can be the basis of a rubric, either in a simple form, such as that shown in Figure 8.1, or in a somewhat more advanced form, as shown in Figure 8.2. This alternative rubric form uses a Likert-type scale from 1 (seldom) to 4 (usually), which argues for finer discrimination along the qualitative continuum.

References at the end of this chapter and resources listed at the back of the book include additional sources of information about making and using rubrics for various grade levels. Of course, rubrics can be quite complex and detailed, especially when they are used in formal evaluation. But instructional rubrics should be fairly simple. Otherwise, the teacher will spend more time teaching the rubric than teaching writing.

Follow-up discussions make rubrics more valuable for all students but especially for auditory learners. There are two important discussion times that make this focused analysis device highly useful. The first is during the development of the rubric. Students should discuss the meaning of the various points in the rubric so that they are clear from the outset about what they are to look for in the writing. Students also should discuss and come to common agreement about what is meant by some of the time or by 1 in the qualitative judgment. The qualitative categories are intentionally holistic. It is essential that students internalize a sense of whether writing is effectively organized or ineffectively organized, for example, if they are to learn to write well. That calls for qualitative judgment, which will be sharpened and refined through discussion and practice with rubrics.

The second occasion for discussion occurs after students have used the rubric to analyze a piece of work, such as an outline or a draft. Follow-up discussion is essential. If the only use of the rubric is to read the outline or the draft and put *Xs* in the appropriate boxes, then the exercise will be incomplete. Follow-up discussion should answer the question "What should I do next?" For instance, if the question "Are the ideas or topics sufficiently developed?" elicits an X in the box labeled *some of the time*, then the follow-up discussion should center on how development can be strengthened. For students, this may mean brainstorming or further research or observation. For the teacher, who can use the rubric as a diagnostic tool, such discussion may guide the re-teaching of certain concepts or strategies.

RUBRICS AND THE SAT ESSAY

In the context of this book, rubrics are used for strategic teaching, to focus on characteristics and qualities so that students can learn to write well. Another use of rubrics is to evaluate writing for the purpose of assigning a score or a rating or a grade. Although my emphasis has been on formative evaluation, it may be instructive to include an example of summative evaluation. The newly minted SAT essay exam provides that example.

In 2005 the College Board introduced an essay section on the SAT that uses a prompt. One sample, provided on its Web site, featured a quotation about success and failure, and then asked the test-taker to respond to the ideas in the quotation. For more information, visit www.collegeboard.com.

When students take the SAT, they will have 25 minutes to compose their responses. The scorers, who are trained, experienced high school or college teachers, will not know what scores the others come up with or the students' identities or schools. The scoring will be holistic. Each scorer will rate the essay using a score from 1 (low) to 6. Each score will be associated with certain parts of a rubric. The top score of 6 will mean that the essay is

- effectively and insightfully developed and demonstrates outstanding critical thinking,
- well organized and clearly focused,
- skillful in the use of language,
- varied in sentence structure,
- free of most errors in grammar, usage, and mechanics.

A variety of instructionally focused rubrics can be drawn from such holistic-assessment rubrics. For example, development and critical thinking might have several instructional components. These could be framed as evaluations of whether a writer:

- maintains a consistent, appropriate point of view;
- demonstrates critical thinking by using clear, focused examples;
- gives reasons and evidence to support his or her position.

By breaking more general statements of writing characteristics into bite-size components the teacher can, in a sense, work backward to the instructional focal points that will be needed in order for students to become effective writers according to this type of summative-assessment rubric.

CONCLUDING THOUGHTS AND A FINAL CHECKLIST

The focus of this book has been to examine ways that teachers can effectively teach visual, auditory, and kinesthetic learners to write well. Learning to write well is important not only because students must demonstrate mastery in order to clear a number of academic and career hurdles, such as passing graduation exams, scoring high on standardized tests (for example, the SAT), and writing convincing college admission essays. Writing well also is important because the act of writing drives the thinking process and vice versa. Indeed, a number of scholars and practitioners have written about the symbiotic relationship between thinking and writing, most coming solidly to the conclusion that the process of writing clarifies thinking and learning, which in turn strengthens writing. A recent and accessible book on this topic is Marlys Mayfield's *Thinking for Yourself: Developing Critical Thinking Skills Through Reading and Writing* (2001). Although the book is geared toward college-level writing instruction, the principles and many adaptable examples make it a worthwhile resource for middle and high school teachers.

Writing instruction too often is given less attention than it deserves in many classes, usually because teaching writing well is time-consuming and challenging, especially if teachers want to reach the visual, auditory, and kinesthetic learners who will likely struggle with writing. Nevertheless, teaching students how to write is vital, as witnessed by the number of books on the market aimed at teaching adults as well as young people how to be effective writers. The title of Laurie Rozakis' *The Complete Idiot's Guide to Writing Well* (2000) in the well-known series is perhaps a backhanded compliment to the importance of effective writing instruction, but the book does acknowledge how important writing is.

Figure 8.3 offers an overview of this book. The closer a teacher can come to checking every item, the more likely the teacher can effectively teach all students, especially visual, auditory, and kinesthetic learners, who, given proper attention to their learning styles, can learn to write well.

Figure 8.3   A Writing Teacher's Self-Assessment Checklist

As a writing teacher, I . . .

- Understand that writing is a multidimensional process and that there is no single correct way to achieve writing success.
- Believe that to teach students to write well I must teach to a variety of intelligences and learning styles.
- Understand that the process of writing consists of responding in various ways to stimuli and that process and product are flexible and interconnected.
- Know that students benefit from understanding their personal learning-style preferences so that they can play to their strengths and take control of their own learning.
- Realize that authentic, purposeful writing assignments connected to students' lives and studies are more motivating than random, made-up assignments.
- Understand that writing fluency comes when students reach automaticity in terms of basic writing processes—and that fluency is a key to writing well in test situations.
- Know that visual, auditory, and kinesthetic learners, in particular, grow by using sense exploration and multisensory observation as writing process tools.
- Understand that *translation* from one form of writing to another is a teachable skill that improves students' ability to achieve automaticity and thus fluency in writing.
- Believe that organizing and drafting can take various forms and that the chosen form should match students' learning strengths or help students enlarge their repertoire of strategies.
- Organize individual, small-group, and whole-class lessons so that students have opportunities to be independent and to collaborate with others.
- Balance direct instruction with taking a role as guide on the side in order to provide students with strategic information and meaningful opportunities to practice using the strategies.
- Incorporate specific visual, auditory, and kinesthetic activities, such as the study of patterns and rhythms, to meet the needs of these learners.
- Know that teaching writing well does not neglect the basics, such as nouns and verbs, but builds on the basics to assist students in gaining sophistication in their writing.
- Use selective correction, rubrics, and discussion in helping students focus their efforts, understanding that, in the end, everything should come together to produce good writing.

Copyright 2006 by Corwin Press. All rights reserved. Reprinted from *Teaching Writing to Visual, Auditory, and Kinesthetic Learners*, by Donovan R. Walling. Thousand Oaks, CA: Corwin Press, www.corwinpress.com. Reproduction authorized only for the local school site or nonprofit organization that has purchased this book.

REFERENCES

Mayfield, M. (2001). *Thinking for yourself: Developing critical thinking skills through reading and writing*. Fort Worth, TX: Harcourt College Publishers.

Rozakis, L. (2000). *The complete idiot's guide to writing well*. Indianapolis, IN: Alpha Books.

Resources

An exhaustive list of print and online resources would fill another book. The following resources are a sample of the excellent books and Internet sites that can assist teachers as they help their visual, auditory, and kinesthetic learners learn how to write well.

PRINT

Arter, J. A., & McTighe, J. (2000). *Scoring rubrics in the classroom: Using performance criteria for assessing and improving student performance.* Thousand Oaks, CA: Corwin.

Blasingame, J., & Bushman, J. H. (2004). *Teaching writing in middle and secondary schools.* Englewood Cliffs, NJ: Prentice-Hall.

Calkins, L. (1994). *The art of teaching writing.* Portsmouth, NH: Heinemann.

Davis, J., & Hill, S. (2003). *The no-nonsense guide to teaching writing: Strategies, structures, and solutions.* Portsmouth, NH: Heinemann.

Dornan, R. W., Rosen, L. M., & Wilson, M. (2003). *Within and beyond the writing process in the secondary English classroom.* Boston: Allyn & Bacon.

Ewald, W., & Lightfoot, A. (2002). *I wanna take me a picture: Teaching photography and writing to children.* Boston: Beacon.

Fiderer, A. (1999). *40 rubrics and checklists to assess reading and writing (grades 3–6).* New York: Scholastic.

Flynn, L. A., & Flynn, E. M. (2004). *Teaching writing with rubrics: Practical strategies and lesson plans for grades 2–8.* Thousand Oaks, CA: Corwin.

Gardner, H., & Checkley, K. (1997). The first seven and the eighth: A conversation with Howard Gardner. *Educational Leadership, 55*(1), 8–13.

Glass, K. T. (2004). *Curriculum design for writing instruction: Creating standards-based lesson plans and rubrics.* Thousand Oaks, CA: Corwin.

Graves, D. (1994). *A fresh look at writing.* Portsmouth, NH: Heinemann.

Mariconda, B. (2001). *Step-by-step strategies for teaching expository writing.* Jefferson City, MO: Scholastic.

Olson, C. B. (2002). *The reading/writing connection: Strategies for teaching and learning in the secondary classroom.* Boston: Allyn & Bacon.

Portalupi, J., & Fletcher, R. (2001). *Nonfiction craft lessons: Teaching information writing K–8.* Portland, ME: Stenhouse.

Ruddell, M. R. (2000). *Teaching content reading and writing* (3rd ed.). New York: Wiley.

Soven, M. I. (1998). *Teaching writing in middle and secondary schools: Theory, research, and practice.* Boston: Allyn & Bacon.

Tompkins, G. E. (2003). *Teaching writing: Balancing process and product* (4th ed.). Englewood Cliffs, NJ: Prentice-Hall.

Warner, M. L. (2000). *Winning ways of coaching writing: A practical guide to teaching writing grades 6–12.* Boston: Allyn & Bacon.

ONLINE

http://grammar.ccc.commnet.edu/grammar

Guide to Grammar and Writing. This site is sponsored by the Capital Community College Foundation in Connecticut. It provides more than 400 resource sections on aspects of grammar and writing suitable for middle and high school writers.

http://www.ipl.org/div/aplus

Internet Public Library, A+ Research and Writing for High School and College Students. This site provides a guide to writing research papers and links to information about writing and composition strategies.

http://www.powa.org

Paradigm Online Writing Assistant. Sections of this site address discovering what to write, organizing, drafting, revising, editing, and so on. Other pages describe types of writing and provide examples.

http://www.readwritethink.org

Read, Write, Think. This site is sponsored by the International Reading Association, the National Council of Teachers of English, and other entities. It provides access to practices and resources for reading and language arts instruction for all grades.

http://www.wisc.edu/writing/Handbook/index.html

The Writing Center at the University of Wisconsin–Madison. This site is an online writer's handbook. The information is intended for college students but is suitable for high school students.

Index

Accountability, 70
Activity-based brainstorming, 37–38
Agnew Clinic, The (Eakins), 64
American Heritage Dictionary of the English Language, The, 93
Artistic mind, 2
Artistic organization, 59–60
Art of Thought, The (Wallas), 24
Asimov, Isaac, 26, 27
Assembly-line writing, 6–7
Assignments, 70
Auditory learning
  information response, 1
  kinesthetic translation, 80
  metaphors, 50
  multidimensional response, 30
  paragraph walkabouts, 67–68
  patterns/rhythms, 76
  pearls-on-a-string organization, 48
  physical walkabouts, 64
  reportage, 35–37
  sensory reportage, 30
Authentic writing
  choice sample, 30
  collaborative aspects, 69
  definition, 19
  response as sample, 28–30
  school writing vs., 20–21
  sensory reportage, 45–46
Automaticity, 25

Bloom, B. S., 25, 42–43, 57, 63
Brainstorming, 37–38
Brain theory, 9
Brevity, 81–83, 97
Browser's Dictionary, A (Ciardi), 93–94

Buckley, W. F., Jr., 25, 27
Buddhism, 24

Ciardi, J., 93
Clarity of thought. *See* Fluency
Clelland, M., 30
Collaborative writing
  authentic writing and, 69
  ground rules, 69–70
  planning, 68–70
  teachers' role, 70–71
College Board. *See* Scholastic Assessment Test I (SAT I)
Complete Idiot's Guide to Writing Well, The (Rozakis), 112
Comprehension, 42
Conceptual density, 81–83
Consciousness, 24–25
Correction, selective, 104–106
Costa, A., 9–10
Creativity, 19–20

Deductive organization, 50–53
Demonstration focus, 108
Description
  auditory, 36
  checklist strategies, 43–45
  third-person, 35
Differentiated instruction, 8–10
Drafting, 68–70

Eakins, Thomas, 64
Eisner, E., 8
Elaboration, 81–83
Enlightenment, 24
Evaluation, Blooms' taxonomy, 42

Factual reportage, 57–58
Fluency, 26–28
Focus, 107–108
Forward progress, 98

Gardner, Earle Stanley, 25
Gardner, H., 10
Garger, S., 9
Gettysburg Address (Lincoln), 75
Gibson, Walter B., 26, 27
Grant, Maxwell, 26
Gregorc, Anthony, 9
Gregory, G., 9, 17
Ground rules, 69–70
Groups, establishing, 69
Guild, P. B., 9

Hamlet (Shakespeare), 97
Hanson, J. R., 9
Hemingway, Ernest, 27
Hodgson, M., 29

"I Have a Dream" Speech (King),
    76, 78–79
Illumination, 24
Incubation, 24
Inductive organization, 50–53
Information gathering, 58–59
Information organizing, 58–59
Informed spontaneity, 62
Instruction, differentiated, 8–10
Intelligences, 10
Inverted pyramid organization
    description, 53–54
    example, 54
    key ideas, 55–57

James, Henry, 26–27
Jung, Carl, 9

Kallick, B., 9–10
Kennedy, John F., 76
Kinesthetic learning
    auditory translations, 80
    learning, 1
    metaphors, 50
    multidimensional response, 30
    paragraph walkabouts, 67–68
    patterns/rhythms, 78

pearls-on-a-string organization, 48
physical walkabouts, 64–65
reportage, 37–38
visual translations, 80
King, Martin Luther, Jr., 76, 78–79
Knowledge, 42
Kolb, David, 9

Learning styles
    auditory (*See* Auditory learning)
    differentiated instruction, 8–10
    kinesthetic (*See* Kinesthetic learning)
    self-assessment, 13–17
    situation-specific, 5
    visual (*See* Visual learning)
Leaves of Grass (Whitman), 8
Lincoln, Abraham, 75
Linear process writing
    characterization, 7–8
    components, 11–12
    implications, 6
    misconceptions, 5
    rigidity of, 6–7
    suitability, 2
    writing as, 5
London, Jack, 29
Lowry, D., 9

Mayfield, M., 112
McCarthy, B., 9
Mental/physical interaction, 25–27
Metacognition, 71
Metaphors
    adaptable, 51–52
    auditory, 50
    kinesthetic, 50
    organizational, 48–49
    visual, 50
Model for Teaching Writing (Walling), 2
Multidimensional responding
    choice sample., 30
    description, 21–22
    response as sample, 28–30
Multiple intelligences, 10

National Association for the
    Advancement of Colored People
    (NAACP), 94
Nouns, 89–91

O'Bannon, A., 30
Observation, 45–46
On Writing Well (Zinsser), 25
Organization
    artistic, 59–60
    deductive, 50–53
    inductive, 50–53
    information, 58–59
    inverted pyramid, 53–58
    metaphors, 48–49
    pearls-on-a-string, 47–50
Outlines, 83–85

Paragraph walkabouts
    analysis, 73–74
    description, 66–68
    sense exploration and, 71–72
Parish, P., 30
Pasteur, Louis, 73–74
Patterns
    adjusting, 76–80
    auditory learners and, 76
    brevity and, 81–83
    conceptual density and, 81–83
    discerning, 76–80
    elaboration and, 81–83
    impact, 75–76
    sample lesson, 87–88
    visual learners and, 76
Pearls-on-a-string organization, 47–50
Planning, collaborative, 68–70
Political correctness, 94–95
Portfolios, 106–108
Preparation, 24
Presentation focus, 108
Process, internalized, 62
Process phase
    choice sample., 30
    consciousness, 24–25
    description, 23–24
    elaboration, 25
    mental/physical interaction, 25–27
    response as sample, 28–30
    speed, 25
Process writing. *See* Linear
        process writing
Products, writing, 12
Projects, focus, 107–108
Pyramid. *See* Inverted pyramid

Rauscher, W. V., 26
Reading, 22–23
Redundancy, 98
Reportage
    auditory, 35–37
    factual, 57–58
    kinesthetic, 37–38
    sensory, 33–34, 45–46
    visual, 35
Revision, 68–70, 85–86
Rey, H. A., 30
Rey, M., 30
Rhythms
    adjusting, 76–80
    auditory learners and, 76
    brevity and, 81–83
    conceptual density and, 81–83
    discerning, 76–80
    elaboration and, 81–83
    impact, 75–76
    sample lesson, 87–88
    visual learners and, 76
Rozakis, L., 112
Rubrics
    advanced, 110(figure)
    definition, 108
    making, 109
    power of, 109
    SAT essay and, 111–112
    using, 109–111

SAT. *See* Scholastic Assessment
        Test I (SAT I)
Satori, 24
Scholastic Assessment
        Test I (SAT I), 111–112
School writing
    authentic writing vs., 20–21
    definition, 19
    motivation, 21–23
*Second Browser's Dictionary,
    A* (Ciardi), 94
Selective correction, 104–106
Self-assessment, 13–17, 113
Seneca, 89
Sense exploration
    paragraph walkabouts, 71–73
    steps, 40–42
    template, 40–41(figure)

Sensory pathways, 9
Sensory reportage, 33–34, 45–46
Shadow, The (Grant), 26
Shortcut slang, 98
Silver, H., 9
Simenon, Georges, 26, 27
Spelling, 99–100
Sprenger, M., 9
Sternberg, R., 10
Stimulus, writing, 10–11
Strategy focus, 108
Strong, R., 9
Synthesis, 42

Taxonomy, Blooms, 42–43
Tests, 7
Thinking
    clear (*See* Fluency)
    consciousness, 24–25
    elaboration, 25
    framework for, 24–27
    modes of, 9
    speed, 25
Thinking for Yourself (Mayfield), 112
Third Browser's Dictionary, A (Ciardi), 94
Third-person description, 35
Thurber, James, 68
Townsend, C., 30
Transcription, 7
Translation
    auditory and visual, 80
    different forms, 38–39
    factual reportage, 57–58
    process, 33–34
Triarchic intelligence model, 10
Trollope, Anthony, 25, 26

Verbs, 89–91
Verification, 24–25
Visual learning
    information response, 1
    kinesthetic translation, 80
    metaphors, 50
    multidimensional response, 30
    patterns/rhythms and, 76
    reportage, 35

Walkabouts
    auditory learners, 64
    description, 62
    kinesthetic learners, 64–65
    paragraph, 65–67, 71–74
    physical, 62–65
    sense exploration and, 71–73
    teachers applying, 62–65
Wallas, G., 24–25
Walling, D., 2, 11, 40
White, S., 4
Whitman, Walt, 8, 12
Words
    basic, 89–91
    choosing, 101–102
    correct choices, 91–95
    easily confused, 92(figure)
    politically correct, 94–95
    reviewing, 100–101
    spelling, 99–100
Wordy phrases, 98(figure)

Zen Buddhism, 24
Zinsser, W., 25

CORWIN PRESS

The Corwin Press logo—a raven striding across an open book—represents the union of courage and learning. Corwin Press is committed to improving education for all learners by publishing books and other professional development resources for those serving the field of PreK–12 education. By providing practical, hands-on materials, Corwin Press continues to carry out the promise of its motto: **"Helping Educators Do Their Work Better."**

Franklin Pierce College Library

00161023